ACKNOWLEDGMENTS

Apologies to my long-suffering wife for the endured hours of enforced silence usually culminating with a "Say that again dear – I wasn't listening."

Thank you to:

My children for pushing me to write it and my friends for enthusing me to just go for it.

My grandchildren for the expectancy and patience for at last seeing grandad in print.

My daughter Sharon for the heritage documentation that sadly I was not able to include in this edition.

My brothers Christian and David for providing background when my memory was in gas-light mode.

Many thanks to my dearly beloved granddaughter Liesje and my good friend Geoffrey for taking the time to proofread the draft copy.

Preface

This book is born from the pressure exerted by my immediate family wishing me to relay the implausible antics my brothers got up to in our childhood, generally with me tagging along, - That's meant to be a get out clause! And while in the mood for slandering the family, I have stoked the fire with fuel by including the unconventional and shady methods my parents took in a bid to survive post WW2.

Throughout I have attempted to accurately record the experiences of my dearly loved parents and their three young rascals. Whilst I vividly recall many, some needed expansion with the help of my siblings. You will find many unbelievable, but I can assure all are true. These tales include a number of tearful occasions, humorous tales in the plenty, as well as an abundance of heart stopping moments.

As a first-time author I rewrote many paragraphs and sometimes pages hoping to provide a creditable result for my family's faith. Once they had received the draft, what I did not expect, but was delighted to hear, was that they all found it difficult to put down.

They then pressured me to publish and distribute the book you have before you now.

I hope you enjoy.

The story begins around the time I was born. Our parents rented the basement and the middle floor of a three-storey detached property in Hornsey, North London. They moved there before I was born so I have relied upon information provided by elder brother Christian for this phase of our lives. He was born about fifteen months before World War Two, whereas both David and I were born during the war years. The blitz was in full swing, with bombs falling from the sky on a nightly basis. To give a measure of safety and security, albeit just limited protection, we slept all together in a Morrison shelter assembled in the basement of the house.

At the back of the house but some way back was the railway that ran from Finsbury Park through Alexandra Park and on to High Barnet.

As part of the home defence the army had Ack Ack anti-aircraft guns strategically placed in a great number of places in and around London and other major cities. To make them mobile and speedily transportable to where they were needed some were mounted onto specially adapted railway trucks. Brother Chris says he can recall these moving along the railway line at the back of us to get to the various vantage positions. Whilst he can recall the Searchlights and boom of the guns he did not see any in action because the family would have been in the Morrison shelter whilst the air raid was on.

My own life began on May 8th. 1942, right in the middle of the war. Mum had been admitted to Hackney Mothers Hospital in East London for care and assistance during the birth.

Mum relayed the story that just when her labour was coming to its climax, the air raid sirens suddenly sounded, putting everyone into safety mode, causing them to rush hither and thither to get the patients into the air-raid shelters, but because her labour was so advanced mum's midwife and doctor stayed at her station to assist with the delivery.

She said that at one point there was an almighty bang that shook the whole building, and she thought the ceiling was about to crash down but fortunately just a shower of dust and flakes of plaster fell down.

I wished I could say this boom was the opening fanfare for the majestic arrival of my own élite birth! But the actual truth is that it was due to a German bomb that had detonated a short distance away.

Although our mum never really said too much about this to us, according to her mum, our Nan, it was a lengthy, tiring, painful process. It was actually an exceedingly difficult birth of twins, which regretfully resulted in the loss of my paired brother within hours. It is one of the many great regrets of my life that I never had a longer discussion with my mum about this. The amazing thing is it was never really mentioned. I have no idea how she felt about losing one of us, although I'm sure she would have been devastated and tearful at this loss.

From my point of view, I do occasionally reflect upon how life might have been had I had a kindred spirit sibling and how he would have steered our lives and quite possibly in a totally different direction.

At some time during the birth, a piece of classical music, 'Blue Danube' began playing on the radio in the labour ward, apparently it had a calming effect on her as well as those assisting her. Such was the timing of the rendition of this beautiful piece of music that it then became mum's all-time favourite.

The trauma of losing one of us is possibly the reason mum immediately bonded with this moving composition, because forever thereafter, if it was played anywhere, it seemed to provide solace and allowed her a few moments of reflection on what might have been, such that the music stayed locked in her heart for the rest of her life.

Whilst, as you can see, it had great meaning for her, it has poignant meaning for me too. Such was her lifelong love of this piece, set deep into her heart that if it played anywhere within ear shot, and I was close by, mum would seek me out, come to me, put her arms around me and we would embrace for the duration of that rendition. Nothing was said, it was just a time for our own private moments of reflection. I have not heard it for a while, however whenever it is played, it takes but a few notes for me to register recognition and it then triggers emotive thoughts within me, such the sentiment takes over and I become immersed in recalling those incredibly special moments with my beloved mum.

I do have to say, although I survived, I was left as a very frail child and remained so from infancy right through to puberty. I do have to say though that I am the last person to want to dwell upon illness. That is that out of the way, so we won't have to mention it again except if it has relevancy.

As I have intimated that era in time did itself produce some instances worthy of mention.

One of those that Mum recalled to me, is a story about when she was heavily pregnant with David.

She had left Chris and me with her mum, whilst she went to do a bit of shopping locally.

She was in one of the shops when the air-raid warning siren suddenly started. Naturally the shop closed immediately so that the staff and customers could seek out an air raid shelter. The nearest convenient to mum being Turnpike Lane tube station and she was rushing as best she could in her current state of pregnancy when she heard the sound overhead.

The reason for the siren turned out to be not for aeroplanes but for a V1 rocket ("doodle-bug"), Hitler's deadly new weapon. As she rushed towards the shelter, she suddenly saw it coming in her general direction, and soon realised that it was about to pass over the area where we lived. She said this made her stop dead in her tracks, while she just stood, held her breath and watched as this latest creation from Hitler's armoury flew noisily overhead towards her. Now totally gripped by fear for her family, overcome with trepidation and with her heart pounding, she continued watching as it moved towards her through the sky and then thankfully on and beyond our home and then move above and past where she stood. Believing that danger had passed her, she was able to breathe again. But with unease as she continued to watch, with her thoughts instead moving to those lives that would be devastated when this murderous monster finally hit a target.

Overcome by the mesmerizing sight of this flying bomb, as if in a trance, she very slowly and aimlessly meandered toward home, when suddenly she realised the distinctive roar of the rocket motor had stopped. Snapping out of her daze, she again began to panic because, without its propulsion this rocket-controlled bomb would fall rapidly from the sky and crash not too far from where she stood, and upon impact devastate a large section of our local community.

The explosion would be catastrophic and totally overwhelm a whole group of ordinary everyday people going about their daily lives. The extent of this devastation would destroy them well beyond their physical loss. Besides making the survivors homeless it would leave them with mental scars that would remain with them for the rest of their lives.

Knowing the danger was not yet over and there was now no chance of getting to the air-raid shelter she began to panic again. She then became aware that a bus-driver had been shouting at her to come to him, snapping back into reality, she ran across the road to join him, the conductor, and a number of passengers as they crawled underneath the bus for 'safety'.

However, I'm not sure that form of shelter would have been very effective against a V1 rocket powered bomb anyway!

Evidently, they laid there and waited and waited for the explosion that never came. It seems it was another of the many duds. This one had landed less than a mile away but having gone nose first into a playing field it had failed to explode. Just as well really because as you will learn as we continue with this tome, the main subject of these tales, brother David, would have been lost and I would not then have that much to write about.

When everyone felt safe, they gradually crawled from under the bus, dusted themselves down, thanked their lucky stars, wished everyone good luck and went on their way. Mum said that it was then that she realised that she was covered in dirt, dust and grime and looked a completely sorry state. Self-conscious of her highly dishevelled appearance she quickened her pace for home, aware she looked more like a down-and-out, and hoped not to meet anybody she knew.

It seems when she got home still feeling rather shaken up by the whole incident and incredibly pleased to again be close to her family, threw her arms around them and immediately burst into tears. Nanny was very concerned to see her daughter bedraggled and in a distressed state, and at first thought she had been attacked. Once mum recovered enough to explain, Nan remained somewhat bemused by the explanation because she had not heard the scream of the air-raid siren or the roar of the V1 rocket motor going overhead.

They were of course completely unaware at that time that the reason the V1 had failed to ignite was that it had met a soft target. They did not find this out until a day or so later when the local gossip was of how lucky they had been because the rocket had landed nose first into the local playing field. They were all incredibly thankful and dread what the result might have been had it hit a building instead.

My own earliest actual recollection was my third birthday, May 8th, 1945. The fact that I can remember my third birthday may seem a bit farfetched to some, but if the penny has not yet dropped the date is significant in that it was the day World War Two ended – VE Day.

Anyway, let us get back to my third birthday. There were literally hundreds of people gayly milling around, the majority of which were going wild with excitement, waving flags and hugging and kissing each other and generally going delirious. There was even a bonfire right there in the middle of the road with people dancing jubilantly around it.

Suddenly a woman snatched me up to join in with the festivities. I was nowhere near as enthusiastic as the crowd, and in fact bawled my eyes out at this intrusion to my personal space. Mum quickly grabbed me back into her arms and skipped back onto the pavement to join in with the celebrations but being aware of the exuberance of other she stayed in very close proximity and protection of her young family.

Taking on the mood of the moment she swirled me and Chris round and round in joy and generally joined in the fun. David was in his pram and slept through it all. It was a period of sheer joy for everyone here and in many other parts of the world that had been freed from Hitler's tyrannous regime. Although the war with Japan continued for another five months after the celebrations had subsided here.

I'm unable to say whether the photo shown here was taken on the day or not but possible soon after because as you can see the bunting and fairy lights are out. What I can say is it was not taken outside our house because to this day I also have photo of that property in my personal photo library.

This now totally bald and wrinkly old coot did at that time have a mop of golden blond hair which as you can see was set in natural tight curls.

I have to say this was possibly why this celebratory throng were joyfully attracted to the little cherub that was me, and who can blame them!

At the magical age of three years old, surely I can be forgiven for thinking it was just my tremendously good looks and undeniable loveable charm that warranted this extremely elaborate birthday party.

I do have to add though, being that popular with the ladies was, I'm afraid, just a one off, never again was I that popular.

My next recollection was a little over a year later and certainly nothing to celebrate, indeed it could not have been more in variance to my previous 'party', because it was an extremely traumatic and harrowing experience for a four-year-old and the entire reason I can remember it to this day.

It was 1946, the war was then part of a not-so-distant past era. Dad, along with two friends as business partners, had purchased a defunct car repair workshops and garage that had ceased to trade as a consequence of the war. This was just off the sea front in Lancaster Road, Great Yarmouth, Norfolk

We as a family were about to move into this new phase of our lives. We obviously needed somewhere to live, and we were at what was soon to be our future abode in Southtown, Great Yarmouth. Although I cannot be certain, I think this visit might have been our preliminary viewing of the property.

I cannot recall going around the house itself at that time, what I do remember so vividly was following along behind Mum, Dad and Chris as we went into the garden. Two-year-old David was probably being carried. As we all went further and further into the 'garden', which was in fact more like a field. The height of the grass and weeds got progressively taller until it was not very long before they were well above my head and totally engulfed me and from my viewpoint the rest of the family was then well out of sight. I soon became disorientated and not knowing which way to go or turn, went into panic mode.

I cannot now recall what I imagined was about to happen to me, but maybe I was terrified that a tiger was about to come through the undergrowth, or perhaps I considered that I had just been abandoned and would never see the family again. Who knows what goes through a four-year old's mind when panic sets in? It must have been totally unbearable thoughts on my part, because apparently, I did make an awful lot of noise and it was some time before I could be consoled.

My reaction was totally OTT even though Dad had gathered me up within seconds of me starting to scream.

OK, so I was a wimp of the first order! Not just in this instance either, but many, many times after. This is totally true and no exaggeration. I was frightened of my own shadow. A very shy retiring child that would not say boo to a goose. A child that clung to mummy's dress should anybody as much as smile in my direction.

I wouldn't even go down a playground slide, swing on a swing or even, god forbid, go up and down on a seesaw because it would have meant being at least a few inches from the ground. These totally normal child activities that gave untold pleasure to most children absolutely terrified me. Any motion sensations which other kids consider great fun, turned me into a quivering wreck at just the thought of stepping on to any one of them. I could not be encouraged to join in any of these absolutely senseless pastimes no matter how many ice creams I was offered. Even with an attempt to bribe me with a candyfloss which I loved, you still would not have been able to get me to as much as sit on one for a photo, even if it was completely stationery and bolted down. Some things that made me tremble with terror are very mundane ordinary daily items like not going near the window on the first floor of a department store because it gave me vertigo as did walking down Great Yarmouth Britannia pier because I could see the sea beneath the minute gaps between the wooden planks!!

This wuss like behaviour of mine did not apply to my brother David though. Far from it, he was and still is, a born daredevil. He was the original stunt man in nappies. If it were dangerous, he would try it and whilst watching him I would slowly sink to my knees, curl into a ball with clenched fists drawn tightly to my cheeks, lay there quivering with trepidation because I was sure this was about to be his last action in this life. I would literally scream at him to stop, please stop, but he would simply stare at me with an incredulous look, utter something demeaning and carry on anyway. He appeared not to have any fear at all throughout his entire life. Mum did say that the pleasure of seeing David take his first steps soon change to one of constant fear as he attempted to become an Olympic sprinter just a day or so after he first learnt to walk. He would take maybe two paces, attempt to run, but would immediately trip and end up head butting a piece of heavy wooden furniture. That used to make him blink for a few seconds before he got up and did it all again.

Although in his very senior years his antics have become slightly more demure. I said slightly!

There are many more tales of his exploits to come, so don't think of putting the book down and turning the light out just yet!

Despite my earlier trauma the family bought and moved into to the house in 1946 and Dad and business partner Robert (Bob) Rilling proceeded to set up the Garage and Workshop, which had closed down in the very early part of the war. Bob lived with us for a bit, but I only have a very faint recollection of him. Uncle Bill, mum's younger brother, having by then been demobbed from the Army, and looking for work, joined the firm as a car mechanic soon after the garage was up and running. As a result, working inside a garage workshop repairing cars for him was understandably a far better deployment than previous. There with the battle of war raging all round him, he would have among many other vital tasks, changed tank tracks whilst laying in a muddy field one day or the beating sun another, all in an attempt to get it back into combat.

My Dad and his co-director Bob were academically trained mechanical and electrical engineers with management experience which fortunately meant they were needed for the war effort. They were drafted to factories making military equipment and components. Dad was fortunately assigned to a factory close to home in London. It might seem a soft assignment compared to the blood and thrust of battle however, although a civilian, he was also enlisted as a reserve fireman.

This did mean that during the height of the blitz, with hundreds of bombs falling each night he would be part of a crew futilely attempting to stop his part of North London that had not been flattened by bombs from burning down instead.

Mum did say that there were days, nay weeks, where he would fall into bed in the small hours and be up again in a couple of hours to go to the day job then do it all again at night.

When I mentioned it to him at some time he said, *"I was one of the lucky ones. OK it was bloody hard exhausting work, but I got home to my family most nights. Just think of all those other poor blighters fighting this war in far flung places that were having it a lot worse and many did not get to come home for years and for far too many, never."*

Having given you an insight into our lives during the war years I will now return to the period when we were all living in Great Yarmouth. A time that I have first-hand knowledge of and can reflect upon with greater accuracy.

I will not come as a surprise to you to learn that throughout the war years and even in late 1946 all coastal areas of Great Britain remained heavily fortified. I imagine the tradespeople in seaside towns like ours could not wait for the beaches to be made available. For many this was really their only means of making a living. The various authorities would have been a under a great deal of pressure to make the beaches and associated local amenities available as soon as possible. Having now been released from the traumas of war, it's likely most people would have wanted to go away on holiday so that they could unwind and put all that behind them.

Whilst researching this book, I was browsing the internet trying to find when exactly Great Yarmouth beach was opened to the public, so that the kids could get their buckets and spades out again.

It took a while to find the clue and I have to say I was a little surprised to come across the answer in an archive copy of the Eastern Daily Express which quoted:

"The Central Beach at Great Yarmouth was opened to the public at 5pm on Friday, 13th July 1946' - a statement prompting the author to note, wryly: *'One wonders if superstitious people waited until the next day...'* – Note it was Friday 13th.

The opening of the beaches and the return of holiday makers and visitors was crucial to the success of the garage as well as the various entertainment venues locals relied upon for their livelihoods.

One of these amusement facilities was the boating lake along the sea front. Dad's garage carried out the maintenance for the little motorboats which visitors could hire to 'putt putt' around the lake for 10 minutes or so, until interrupted by the now familiar shout *"Come in number xx, your time is up."*

One great advantage to dad's garage deal with the boat owner was that we as a family all became well known to him, such that even when it was busy, we could just turn up and always managed to jump the queue and get a totally untimed 'freebee' much to the irritation of those that had been queueing for ages.

I have a clear recollection of us all in one of these little boats motoring around the boating lake. Which must mean one of two possibilities, one, perhaps I'd been given a sedative pill, or two, maybe it was that the promise of an ice-cream did work occasionally.

The garages reputation for being able to repair most things mechanical meant there were other facilities including some on the Pier that were on call.

One of those was the "carousel". This would have meant being spun around, so obviously having centrifugal force unwillingly applied to by body was not a ride I would even consider, but David and Chris again both loved it.

I do have to say that it was extremely boring to be left to just stand there watching them while I was thinking *"How can anybody in their right mind enjoy that."*

It seemed that the decision to open a garage to repair and service cars, vans and the odd truck or two had been a wise decision. With very few other garages open at that time, Dad and Uncle Bill always seemed very busy. Whereas Bob had to be encouraged to join in even if that did mean he might have to allow grease to get under his fingernails. Although good friends for many years, Dad soon found out Bob was not a keen practitioner of working for a living. It seems there were always invoices to be calculated and written up and suppliers to be paid that would keep Bob busy all day given the chance. Mum helped out at the garage too, probably doing the paperwork, so that Dad could drag Bob screaming and shouting to the workshop and get him to actually pick up a spanner. Mum did at some time say that Bob was far better at talking about things than actually doing them, which leads me to surmise he did not rate very highly in her book.

Many years later I was at a family function and sat for a chat with Uncle Bill. The conversation got round to his time at the garage. He mentioned that Bob, who was the son of a successful businessman, had a la-de-da voice but would attempt to mimic a cockney accent to take the mickey out of Bill's London working class beginnings. He said that did not bother him, but what did, was Bob snapping orders at him like a sergeant major. Bill said in response he would click his heels to snap to attention and reply with a *"Yes Sir"* and emphasise this with a well-rehearsed full salute, just like the army.

He added that Bob only did this when Dad was not around because he would have ripped him to bits. Bill also said that Bob considered himself the "technician" of the business, such that when "working" he would try hard to spend all his time tinkering under the bonnet until the heavy dirty work was finished. Dad told Bill he preferred this rather than have it on his conscience, should Bob have ever humiliated himself enough to crawl under a car and fit new brake shoes to a customer's car!

Dad and Bob met when they were in their late teens so, as I say, had been friends for a considerable number of years. They had been great motorbike enthusiasts and travelled over a great deal of England, Wales and even to the Isle of Man for the TT races.

I had two whole photo albums of their motorcycle touring exploits which I digitised so that I could have an easily accessible permanent record available if wanted.

Among these photos are some with mum and dad all goggled up and in leathers posing at a variety of signpost points in this country as well as places of interest. It seems that in those carefree days before they were married they would pack some sandwiches and a flask, point to a place on a map and head there most weekends along with the rest of the motorcycle clique.

All of the group were from financially sufficient families, so expenditure for niceties like motorcycles, leathers, and such accessories as well as exploratory trips to far flung districts were well within their budget.

The motorcycles were all top of the range machines complete with all the modifications available at the time. Dads was a bit of a rarity in that it was a Scott three-cylinder 750 c.c. water cooled machine. Which apparently drew the attention of other motorcycle enthusiasts of the era.

As I will explain later, all of this changed when they got married and the reality of everyday life became the norm. The motorbike was sold to pay for furniture, bedding, and the like.

Getting married did curtail involvement with the majority of the group although they did continue to keep in touch with Bob Rilling and Fred Mahringer and it is this lasting association that eventually led to the purchase of the garage.

I have many recollections of us spending time at the garage. Being given spanners and discarded car parts to take apart, putting things back to where they came from in the stores, with me "Doing paperwork" in the office or us just generally playing.

We spent so much time there that when Dad's sister Auntie Julie heard of it, she made a full set of mechanics overalls for each of us, embroidered with the words R&M Motors and sent these up from London.

As you can see by the photograph a considerable allowance had been made for growth!

I am not sure how he found the spare time, but in the workshop Dad did manage to make us a mock steam locomotive out of a forty-gallon oil drum, a couple of empty oil cans, packing crates, discarded car parts and redundant metal items. Once the engineering had been completed and just before it was handed over as a new plaything for us boys, it was painted up in the LNER colours and to authenticate it, it had a copy of the logo on the side.

As I remember it could hold two of us seated in the cab side by side. It was man, sorry child, powered along by sticking our feet through a hole in the floor and scooting it along.

We did spend a lot of time playing with that, but we needed Chris to be with us, and in the right mood, because at the time he was the only one with legs long enough to scoot it. It did mean that we had to coax him to join in, but remember it was a two-seater, one of us had to just stand and watch, invariably me!

That said I do clearly remember one occasion when Chris was uncooperative, so David thought we could do without him and decided I should put my back up against the rear of the Loco and push it around with him in the cab, feet up and steering.

Which was great for a while until he decided to steer it down the slope in the workshop and on and on straight out into the street. The reason the braking system had failed to work being quite simply that Dave's legs were just too short!

As you can imagine Dad was not impressed one little bit. Although I do have to say that such was the era that he was more likely to have been trampled by a horse and cart than be mowed down by an automobile.

Mind you Automobiles had by then progressed quite a way from being steam powered and were becoming more and more favoured than having to feed, water and stable a horse, so the chance of being minus one child had still been a possibility I suppose.

After that we were not allowed to play with the locomotive unless the workshop sliding door was closed.

Although we seemed to spend a lot of time at the garage, we did also have great fun at home too. Home was a very large double fronted house with a central front door and large square bay windows either side. The entrance lobby was spacious and led you into the hall. Off which were three reception rooms, a kitchen, utility room and toilet. Upstairs there were four exceptionally large bedrooms and a bathroom. In the early days we had a room each.

All bunking in together, I'll leave 'till later.

Out the back of the house was a large garden with a ship lap fence behind flower beds mostly set out with roses along the left flank. The wall on the other side was a flintstone about two and a half metres high.

The garden was the same depth as those of the houses to the left and right of us, but then it widened out to pass around the back of the gardens of these houses, into what can only be described as a field.

This was mainly set out as an orchard with a variety of fruit trees. In the main apple, but also pears, damsons, and plums. The left border was enclosed by an advertising hording which stretched along its full length, the other side of which was Gorleston High Street.

My recollection is that we were incredibly happy in that house and both David and I have very many moments that give us warm feeling inside when our thoughts fall back on them. One of my strong recollections of bedtime was while we were waiting for dad to come home. Once we had all been bathed ready for bed and sitting in our dressing gowns by the range in the kitchen, we would be ready for Mum to read us stories until he came in. The stories were invariably by the brothers Grimm. Many of which were grim indeed! However, I am sure that mum actually placed her own embellishment upon them to dull down the more gruesome detail, because nobody died, they were just made to go to sleep! This was a nightly ritual that we really did look forward to. I have these fond recollections of both of us begging and pleading for just one more until dad had arrived back home, and it usually worked.

Although I do have to say the times he arrived home were set by very flexible timescales. Conscientious as he was, if someone needed their van that day then dad would stay until it was fixed and that meant it could often be late into the evening before he returned.

On the occasions that dad was home before we were tucked up in bed, he would often take over the good night story. But he like to do things his way, so the ritual would be changed to us both being in David's bed. The stories were just a chapter long, no amount of pleading would soften his resolve. It was, book shut, lift me out of David's bed, ruffle his hair, goodnight, shut door, and similarly to me when he put me into my bed. No messing its bedtime.

Whereas, with mum even when we were in bed we could still drag it out a bit and always ended up with a big hug and a kiss too.

By this time, you are possibly wondering why my recollections just revolves around me and David.

Well, as a reminder, Chris was four years older than me and six years senior to David, so the majority of our actions were far too infantile for him. Obviously, his bedtime did not coincide with ours and the tales for our story time were I suppose for 'children' and something he had grown out of a long time since. This will be the theme throughout, Chris was on a different planet to us and had totally different modes of enjoyment to us.

Whereas David and I were inseparable throughout our lives, albeit that he was the dominant one and generally decided which activity was to be next, with my opinion having little or no bearing upon the final choice of our playtime fun.

I have to say that throughout this series of recollections, I can recall a lot more of what us two actually did than I can any that included Chris. I cannot say that Chris was a recluse. He just got his enjoyment doing things more suited to his age and that meant he was out of sight and out of mind most of the time. His great friend was "Jacques" from school. Chris would spend most of his time with him, either at our house or his.

Whilst on this vein, one of the noticeable things, as I recall, is that neither David nor I seemed to have any friends over to our house to play. Save for Graham the Greengrocers son from across the road. I think mum dissuaded us from playing with him. Number one, his language was somewhat crude. I can remember Dave severely chastising him for saying "Bugger". Yes, David giving a course in social etiquette. Now that really does take the biscuit!!

It is true that shortly after Graham arrived, there would be squabbles, or toys would be mistreated or even broken, and mum would say *"I think it's time for you to go home Graham."* In his defence, it must have been difficult being the only child and having to play after school and all-day Saturday in the shop all on his own.

A further hitch to our harmony was his family were from Birmingham, real Brummies', so in truth neither David nor I really understood a word he said, unless it was profanity, in which case we would give him a wide-eyed glare in total disbelief of what he had just uttered! Obviously, Graham liked the taste of soap!

I imagine that after reading through our escapades you are thinking you wouldn't let your children play with us either. Although, I want to believe that the reason we did not have any other friends was quite simply there were not any children close by of our age.

There was of course Margaret, 'Mimi' to us, and who could forget her. Mimi was from next door but one and a bit younger than Dave. It was from her that we learnt that the major difference between boys and girls was not just that girls have longer hair, but far more by her educational habit of preferring to play without her nickers!! Or whipping them off mid play for no apparent reason! A bit of a shock for us boys only just out of infancy.

She was certainly a wild one. We always knew when Mimi was around. Loud does not describe her by any stretch of the imagination. So, she was another one mum actively discouraged us from associating with.

Dave recently reminded me of a time when we were playing "tag" and David went to tag her as she ran by at speed, but he caught her long hair instead, and it became entangled in his fingers with the painful result that a big clump was ripped out, leaving her screaming at the top of her lungs due to the pain.

It was totally accidental I can assure you, but it did cause a bit of a neighbour issue because she told her mum he had done it deliberately.

I still have this frightening memory of her mother beating hell out of our door knocker and mum opening the door to be confronted by a raging bull.

Being unable to get a word in edgeways, mum slammed the door in her face and went off to find David. He obviously protested his innocence. Dave not having a great reputation for innocence then relied upon the George Washington qualities of brother John to relay the real truth of the incident. This was followed by an even greater pounding on Mimi's mum's front door which resulted in a period of 'further discussion' that most certainly must have been heard by the fishermen trawling out on the Dutch coast!

I have to add here that there are many mothers who do eventually realise that they have bred a brood of hooligans, but god forgive anyone else that utters that thought within their mother's earshot.

Anyway, you might ask why didn't we have school friends over to play? The answer is I don't really know. Although, I suppose I should say, we went to a Private Preparatory School just across the road from where we lived which at its height had something like ten pupils the majority of which were girls. Play with girls – don't be silly.

Out of our whole school of ten pupils I can only remember the name of one of the children, a girl called Norma and she was the other member of my class of two. The names of the others are now a total blank sheet in my fast-decaying memory. Mind you, names have never been a strong point with me, whereas numbers, that is another matter. I'm not sure why we never had either of the two boys over or were ever invited to their houses. Mind you, it was most probably just another case when our reputations preceded us.

Our next-door neighbours to our right had a son about our ages, however his dad was a bank manager, and the whole family was somewhat aloof anyway, so obviously our repute had once again failed to impress the neighbours. Contact between us and their son seems to have been totally discouraged and suppressed all meaningful contact between our families. The wall separating us was more like a roman build fortress. It was constructed out of flint-stone and was something like two and a half metres high. This impenetrable structure did in any case make day to day conversation somewhat difficult. David did on at least one occasion manage to climb the wall and attempt to speak to the lad but was told in no uncertain terms by the father to *"get down this instant and do not climb up there again."* David being David, remembering something his mum had remarked about, called back, *"snob",* then to ensure he expressed displeasure equal to that of our *'superior'* neighbour, poked his tongue out and blew a raspberry before jumping down.

Mum said she was on nodding terms with the mother, and that was how it stayed even if they had a chance meeting in the street or even in a shop. Just a nod of the head a "good morning/afternoon" was the sum total of each and every conversation. The father was apparently even less of a conversationalist. In his case a courteous tip of the trilby hat to mum was the total extent of his contact with his neighbour of obvious uncouth parentage.

The couple to the left were quite elderly and the man spent a lot of time gardening. The garden was immaculate, and they would spend time sitting reading and enjoying the fruits of his labours. They were quite friendly and would talk to us quite warmly. However, the man did not like us climbing the fence and would very politely ask us *"Can you please get down because you might fall and hurt yourself or break the fence – That's good chaps"*

I am now forced to go back a bit in time, because I have neglected to mention when I actually started at school. According to my mother, I kept bothering her to let me go to school. Chris, being eight was obviously already at school and in fact says that he also went to Carlton House, however I have no recollection of him being there with me at any time. Anyway, although I was only just four Miss Bensley agreed to take me for the mornings a couple of times a week. One morning mum heard the front door close and had gone to investigate only to find I had sneaked out with my coat on and was about to cross the busy main road.

She rushed out to intercept but was just too late because I was already darting across the road. Mum was horrified to see a car was almost upon me, screamed 'stop', car tyres screeched and fortunately I stopped instantly, much to the relief of the driver and mum's heart. I quickly scooted back on to the pavement. I can still visualise this picture of mum clinging on to our gate post, praying her heart would restart soon and the driver with his head resting on the steering wheel seemingly wishing likewise.

It was only when mum relayed this to Miss Bensley that they agree it would be best to let me go full time. Although, I think I fully recognised my previous peril, because thereafter I always waited until I was taken by the hand and delivered to the school door by mum.

The Photo is of the complete school. David in the middle, with braces of the hold your trousers up type and I'm far left. Carlton House School was just one very large room on the ground floor within a much larger property which at one time had been the county manor house. Miss Bensley is pictured in the centre.

She was a genuinely nice lady who spoke softly and encouraged us to always try to do our best. She never seemed to get cross with us. But could nonetheless be pretty firm when it came to controlling our behaviour and our commitment to study.

In some respects, the school was still set in a time warp. We still used the age-old method of doing arithmetic by working out sums using chalk on a slate.

It is strange the things on can recall from their early years, but one worthy of mentions was that if your stick of chalk had a bit of grit or something in it, it gave a scratchy, screaming, nerve jangling sort of noise on the slate that Miss Bensley was not very fond of at all!

If you ignored this, deliberately or otherwise, it would cause her great annoyance. She would just simply come to you, give you a daggers look, hand you a different chalk and go back to her desk, rub the offending area on a piece of stone to wear away the annoying part and then put the chalk back in the box. She didn't throw the chalk away because it had a cost. Parents school fees covered all expenditure including the writing material and books as well as her meagre personal income.

Even given that this was at post war times when austerity was in full swing, I must say everything in the school was well beyond that and can only be described as archaic. If you have ever watched the Dickens film Oliver or the like, that is what it was like.

 We sat on wooden benches behind our wooden desks. The desk top sloped for us to use as our writing area. It was hinged at the back so that it formed a box into which we put our slate and books.

Set into the top was an ink well and a groove next to that onto which you laid your pen. No, it wasn't quite a quill, similar but it had a metal nib you dipped into the ink. One dip of the nib would allow you to write maybe two or three words before you had to dip again.

This could, well in my case anyway, end up with a totally shambolic mess of more ink blots than written words. I never quite mastered the art of writing with an ink pen onto paper. Dipping the pen into the inkwell and withdrawing it retained some ink in the nib by what is called a capillary action.

However, if you pressed just a little bit too hard when writing the nib would release *all* of the ink in one go and you would end up with a pool of ink, an ink blot, on your paper instead. So, to coin a phrase, and I am sure this phrase was engineered with me in mind, I was always "blotting my copy book". What I could not understand was, at home we had pencils to write and draw with, but Miss Bensley insisted on chalk, pen and ink.

From the school photo you can see she was a very elderly lady and as such was stubbornly stuck in her ways. Her aim appeared to be to make our writing a true art form. To her mind perfect calligraphic penmanship defined a true scholar, a distinction set in a long forgotten bygone age. To her despair, try as we might, neither David nor I could reach even passable mastery in this now long outmoded measure of academic achievement.

Despite close tutoring and studious study to the finer points of calligraphy, sadly it only ever resulted in a very disappointing outcome. However, there were other areas of my education where I faired rather better. Maths and reading being the subjects that I performed best at.

Not long after I started my education with Miss Bensley, a friend of my father had popped in one day and dad was enthusing about how well I was doing at school and how I could already read even though I had only been there a short time.

The friend Basil does no more than hand me the newspaper that he had tucked under his arm and selects a section and simply asks me to read it.

I went very shy and looked at dad hoping he would dig me out of this embarrassment, because I thought he had gilded the lily quite a bit, but he just said, *"Go on – Give it a try"*.

So, I did and at least managed to read most of it although the longer words were a mystery that I needed help with.

Still, I must have impressed, because Basil said *"Well done young man"* in a quite enthusiastic tone and he then patted me on the head.

Dad must have been as proud as he had hoped because he put his arm on my shoulder and pulled me in to him. Now that was not something he did very often at all. Words of praise if warranted, yes, but physical demonstrations of emotion were an exceedingly rare reaction for him for any of his tribe.

I did promise not to dwell on my health, but I do have to say that I did suffer from asthma right from infancy. I mention this because it was only when I was very much older that I was given an allergy test, only to discover that I had a reaction to cats, horses and some foods. However, the reaction to the presence of cats we were not aware of until much later, but it did explain why I could often have asthma attacks come on when I was at school. Eating fish, the odour of them raw or being cooked my parents had quickly become aware of.

Miss B, besides being fond of children was also very fond of cats, such that she had six and these would wander in an out of the classroom every day and loved to be stroked and cuddled. To add to my problems Miss B cooked a lot of fish for herself and the cats. So, there I was studying in a minefield. But to be fair the knowledge of the causes and possible medication for asthma were still largely unknown by the medical profession at the time. It was long after leaving Carlton House School that the reasons for attacks became known and the medication to relieve it was made available.

A number of these attacks were very severe and had me laid off for up to a week or so sometimes. But every cloud has a silver lining as they say, and in my case, there was little more I could do than sit and just read, do arithmetic that mum set and all of this because home study expended little energy.

When I was well enough again Mum would have to take me to the library to find another series of books to read. Mum would have a library card for David and one for Chris which they rarely used, which allowed me to come back with six books sometimes.

You have to remember that in our day, books even if available, were awfully expensive to buy, so the library was the answer to satisfy the yearnings of this junior bookworm.

Another source of enjoyment when I was off school during my sick days was the radio.

I would like to hear 'Listen with Mother' on the radio at lunchtime and before bedtime it was 'Dick Barton Special Agent.' Although there were many other programmes that I liked these two were among my favourites. The titles of the others are now a mystery to me.

I think I mentioned earlier that during our time at Carlton House the number of 'Students' was about ten, but during my six years study there were up to as many as twelve all aged between five and eleven.

There were gaps in class ages, I cannot now say with certainty if there was ever a class of one pupil, but certainly never more than three in any one class.

You may recollect that I said our school was basically one very large shabby old room in an equally dilapidated but large old house. The desks were actually set round this one room with sufficient distance between each to define that area as a "class."

The whole of the classroom was covered in wooden floorboards with no carpet or linoleum, in fact no floor covering whatsoever.

These floorboards were very worn and even though we were obviously all lightweight, they creaked as we walked. In fact, they were that badly worn that I am sure a heavier person would have gone right through them. There was a big, impressive fireplace set along the middle of the wall with a big hearth that was filled with coal and lit in winter to keep us warm and cosy. My desk was up against an outside wall directly facing the fireplace. Between me and the fireplace was an intriguing trapdoor set into the floor, which I'll come back to later.

There was another room just off the classroom which was the music room. Well, I say music room, but in essence it was no more than a room with a piano.

Nevertheless, it did have carpet on the floor and curtains at the window, so quite palatial by comparison to the classroom.

All that said, I'm sorry to say that Miss Bensley's activities were totally limited to educating children, so that when it came to cleaning, lightly flicking a feather duster around and a quick brush of the floor with a broom was the limit of her domestic duties.

The toilets for us children though, were in the garden in a block away from the house and like the whole house these had seen better days.

The budget from school fees did not run to employing a janitorial service, as a result our toilets were always in dire need of very intense cleansing.

I don't think I should elaborate on the subject of toilets any further other than to add that most pupils did learn that to avoid embarrassing moments one needed to develop mind over matter control of their bodily function until they arrived back home.

By now I imagine that your initial thoughts of us having been extremely fortunate and privileged to have been privately educated in a fee-paying preparatory school will by now have waned considerably and been replaced by visions of us having more a Dickensian education to mould our early years.

The school having been the Manor House in an earlier life meant it was still an imposing building, albeit by our time there, showing signs of many years of sheer neglect and in desperate need of maintenance and I mean a great deal more than just an honest lick of paint would enhance.

The entrance to the school was via a few steps leading to a quite ornate leaded stained-glass windows either side of the porch and to the main front door. Beyond the door was a lobby leading to the hallway, the floor of which was finished with ornate leaf patterned tiles.

At the far end of the hallway was the classroom and the staircase to the upper floor was about halfway down. In all our time there none of us ever found out what was upstairs, but with the house's main daytime occupants being children, many speculative theories did abound.

One of which was related to the trapdoor in the floor of the classroom that I mentioned earlier.

This was a continual point of discussion during breaktimes that went on for many months. What was upstairs? What was below the trapdoor? These were mysteries that needed investigation.

What made us even more inquisitive was that Miss Bensley was adamant that it was just a door in the floor and there was nothing the other side.

This normally demure soft-spoken elderly lady would get quite cross if we asked what to us seemed totally innocuous but very pertinent questions. All of which just added fuel to the fire. The eldest girl pupil, whose name I can no longer remember, but let's call her 'Rachel', - Top left in the photograph - was the self-appointed head girl.

She had an incredibly vivid warped imagination and dreamed up many theories that never failed to make the hairs on the back of our necks prickle.

Thoughts like Miss B had two mentally deranged sons that she kept gagged and locked in cages in the attic and only fed them when we had gone home for the day. When we queried why we did not hear them banging about or rattling their cage bars 'Rachel' said the attic was fully soundproofed and that was why they appeared quiet.

All her yarns were outrageous to the extreme, but when narrated by her became totally believable and progressively spooky, such that we remained enthralled even though gripped in terror.

To her mind, when the Lord of the Manor owned Carlton House it had also been the courthouse, where local trials were regularly carried out.

After the due process of the law had been administered, justice often demanded that any convicted prisoners were then chained by arm and leg irons to serve their sentence and thrown into the dungeon, which was below the trapdoor.

She said that unfortunately when the Lord died nobody remembered they were there, so the remaining prisoners just starved to death. She said when she was all alone one day she had opened the trapdoor and cautiously crept down to find to her horror that the remains of the prisoners were still there. They even had their tools of torture manacling their skeletons to the wall and they had been left dangling there like that for more than a hundred years. As you can see 'Rachel' had an overactive imagination and could make up stories at the drop of a hat.

There were many, many more like these but I think you got the gist of her ability to captivate and terrorise the whole school, so I will not indulge you more.

All of this has diverted me from my main purpose which was to outline what was actually below the trapdoor. As I said this topic had been 'Rachels' overriding focus for a while and as time went by she became progressively more adamant that we should 'lift the lid' and expose the truth. Obviously, none of us were too keen on releasing the ghosts of the past.

Well, all except one total sceptic, as you might have guessed, my brother David. When an opportunity arose the rest of us rushed to the other side of the room while he quickly tried to release the sliding bolt, but it appeared to be stuck and before he could move it Miss Bensley was heard returning.

The initial few occasions that he had a chance were quite short and it was not long before the lookout announced, "she's on her way back" and this was far sooner than Dave would have liked.

However apparently, he had managed to move the bolts just a little bit. He did have a couple more attempts but again time closed in on him before he could complete the task.

He became increasingly frustrated and even more obsessed with finding out what was being kept hidden.

But it was only a few days later that a far greater time slot was made available when Miss B announced that her neighbour was ill in bed and that she would have to pop out from time to time to help her.

Miss Bensley, soon announced she would be in her kitchen preparing Mrs. X a meal, so we were told to revise some of our previous work and she would pop back from time to time to check on us.

Whilst she spent her time in the kitchen 'Rachel' the lookout could generally hear her preparing the meal, but at times it went quiet, and she would tap David on the shoulder, and he would have to stop trying to move the bolts because that made noises that were unnatural for those dedicated to scholarly study.

Meanwhile the whole class held bated breath not knowing if Miss was about to return and frustrate our attempts.

Although David made a couple of serious attempts on the bolts, the screech caused by wiggling them, was drowned out by the chopping sounds of Miss's food preparation. His effort was eventually thwarted by the sudden sound of footsteps in the hall and he and 'Rachel' only just got back to their desks. What going on she enquired – *"Nothing Miss"* was the unified reply. *"Well, it's awfully quite in here and that usually means mischief is afoot."*

It was then I noticed that David had got one bolt free, and the other was only just hanging on by millimetres and there was Miss Bensley standing in the middle of this trapdoor that now had very little stopping it from opening and letting her fall in.

I sat at my desk absolutely mortified and praying she would move away before the door gave way and she plunged to her death. Fortunately, she did not look in my direction otherwise my face would have given the game away.

Miss Bensley then said, *"I'm just going to take Mrs X's lunch over to her, I will not be long"* and she was gone. We had heard a number of *"Not long"* promises when Miss was popping over to see Mrs X, which quite often meant that we would enjoy a very much extended play time break.

Things were looking good for our 'tomb opening' escapade. It only took a short amount of time for David to free the other bolt and everyone else darted to the other side of the room in fear of what might be discovered beneath the door.

It came as a complete surprise that the door did not open downward but upward instead.

David, being the only child with enough courage to expose the dungeon attempted to open it.

While all the others cowered in terror he made repeated attempts to lift the trapdoor, but although he tried with all his might it was too heavy for him to lift on his own. He then got really cross with me and made it clear that what a ghost might do to me was nothing compared with what he would do if I didn't assist him.

He also managed to convince 'Rachel', by similar threats, that her effort was required too. It took all three of us straining every sinew in our bodies to lift the trapdoor and all we had managed was to do was to raise it just a few inches, when a loud voice behind us shouted *"And what do you think you are doing!"* and there was the usually mild-mannered Miss B with hands curled into fists pressed against her hips in a very uncharacteristic pose that clearly indicated that she was absolutely livid at our actions.

"Whose idea was this?", she retorted. Initially there was no reply from the ten pupils present. *"I need an answer and I need it now"*, she bellowed which itself indicated the level of her annoyance.

Almost as one, seven pupils pointed out the same culprit – David. Ok he had been caught red handed with his fingers in the pie or should I say the trapdoor.

Miss B. then turned to him and said, *"I might have guessed"*. You can understand why he was outraged at this, with justification I might add, considering that every pupil of the school was involved, and it certainly was not his idea originally. He just happened to be a very willing participant.

This injustice only served to send him into one of his temper rages, threatening all and sundry with serious harm and worse, and he was generally out of control. Being unable to control his outburst Miss Bensley then said, *"David, you are suspended. Go home."* Referring to me, *"And as for you young man, I'm amazed at you for getting involved, you are suspended too, go with him and you too 'Rachel' and rest assured all of you, your parents will be hearing from me shortly."*

46

I knew this would not bode well when Dad became aware, but there was worse to come.

While putting on her coat 'Rachel' was offering a pleading apology, whereas I passively followed along behind David who was still in his rage, he stamped down the hall hoping the noise would demonstrate his displeasure, and out of the building and in sheer fury slammed the front door with such force that the whole building shook. I was initially startled by the bang and then horrified to watch as the stained-glass window left its frame, flew and landed with an ear jangling sound of glass smashing, into a hundred-pieces. This once beautiful example of art now reduced to a forsaken collection of useless multi-coloured glass shards, lay all over the school front path, as the result of one child's temper tantrum. Initially I just stood there transfixed in another of my horrified spells. However, I soon pulled myself together and took what seemed like the only sensible option open to me at that time. Which was to attempt to get as much light between me and the event as possible, so I sprinted to catch David up.

As I caught up with him he was nonchalant and strode off totally unconcerned at the consequence of his protest for justice, even though to me this was a far greater criminal offence than forcibly removing a policeman's headgear. I thought it was sure to end up with us both on a custodial sentence.

I tried to reason with him, but he was in no mood to discuss the result of his actions, which meant I had you use every bit of my persuasive powers and duck a few punches in between, before he agreed that the best option was to just go home and face the music.

After all we were by then totally versed in how this interview was likely to be phrased. The repercussions related to the suspension from school were mild in comparison to Mum & Dad's individual dressing-downs regarding the destroyed window.

I do have to say that Dad did expect the two of us to stand shoulder to shoulder and take the rap equally even though this was another of those occasions when one of the parties involvement in the whole affair had been somewhat minor.

Dad's attempts at reassembling the leaded stained class frame were fruitless and Miss Bensley was indeed gracious in allowing Dad to replace it with a standard frosted glass frame.

Unbelievably, after all of this speculation, trouble, trepidation, and probable punishment we did not ever find out what was actually below that trapdoor.

As a footnote I do have to add that I often wonder if 'Rachel' ever became a famous horror writer, because her ability to totally enthral us all with her 'off the cuff' morbid narrations certainly would have been good groundwork for any book or screenplay that had a horror theme.

At some time, in an attempt to avoid us consistently coming in with muddy feet, Dad decided to concrete over the back garden. Not the orchard area, just the nevertheless still large part immediately outside the back of the house. To this end he purchased an enormous quantity of sand, ballast, and cement.

I cannot remember how it was delivered or if anybody assisted him. Again, I'm not sure how he transported it from outside in the road through the coal cupboard at the side of the house and onward to the back. However he achieved this it was no mean feat, because the heap of sand to us, was the height of a mountain. I do clearly remember the pile of cement sacks, covered over with a tarpaulin, the mound of ballast and the mass of sand.

When he had finished this labour and was back at work, the mountain of sand became our focus and our entertainment for the day.

There we were in our glory having great fun climbing over it, rolling down from it, shovelling it into buckets and making sandcastles and the like. Then we had this incredibly good idea (well to us it was) which was to burrow into this enormous mound and make a cave for us to use as a hiding place.

We set to work and sure enough after an hour or two of toil we had tunnelled out a den into the sand and spent the next few hours pretending to be cave dwellers of ancient times. We were a little disappointed in that from time to time small sections of the roof would fall down on us and we had to keep clearing this.

When Dad arrived home, we could not wait to show him the fruits of our labour and eagerly took him by the hand to show him our cave.

He immediately screamed for mum to come there and really gave all of us an almighty dressing down for our sheer stupidity.

What we were too young to appreciate was that it was only because the sand was damp that it stayed together and allowed us to shape it.

Had the roof totally collapsed, and it was only a miracle that it had not, with the weight of the sand upon us, meant we certainly would not have had a chance to move, let alone dig ourselves out.

Mum could have probably been busy and not even noticed the collapse until it was far too late to assist us. Even if she had she probably would not have been able to remove sand quickly enough to stop us both from suffocating.

Dad's normal manner when chastising us was generally one of a firm but calm explanation to the reasons it was not acceptable.

However, on this occasion he became incredibly agitated and loud, and I have to say fearsome in his argument. It is only now that I understand that this uncharacteristic, heated outburst was probably due to his intolerable vision of what might have happened if the roof had collapsed with us in it.

What is true is that even forceful explanations of what might be the outcome of our stupidity, it never seemed to make us stop and think first.

It is probably somewhere about now that you are wondering how I can remember all these tales, to which I say it is that now that I have got well in to writing this narrative, they are coming back to me faster than I can write them down.

So much so that I am now compiling a list of short notes and add new ones immediately they come to me. At this moment I have only relayed about a quarter of our antics from the list.

Let's move on. I must say that looking back I have this unrealistic thought that the sun was always shining and that we spent all our time outside, whereas the reality was probably that the weather then was much the same as it is today.

I say this because nearly all my recollections are of us playing, or probably more accurately, being mischievous, in good weather, within the vast outside expanse that was our play area.

On one of these perpetual sunny days, we had found a largeish cardboard box lying around.

David climbed into it and closed the lid. Just then mum, who had obviously not seen his coverup, came along with breadcrumbs for the birds, *"Where's David"* she enquired, *"Don't know"* I replied exploiting my best RADA trained acting.

She carried on breaking up the bread for a moment then said *"Can you go and find him. I don't like it when he's quiet. It usually means he's up to no good"* At that moment David burst from his captivity with a big *"BOO"*. Mum literally jumped out of her skin.

Her shock was that great that she staggered and sat down backwards, somewhat heavily, rather ungainly, and clutching her heart. Whereas I was genuinely concerned for mum and rushed over to try to help her get up, David just curled up in fits of laughter. After a few seconds Mum also burst out laughing and that set me off too so that we all ended up splitting our sides with laughter. Ok, it's not much of a tale but I have relayed this just to show how sometimes it can be just the smallest of memories that can live with you forever.

It might have been the same day and possibly the same cardboard box and breadcrumbs. As I have already mentioned it was a beautiful sunny day and there we were playing with a cardboard box, when we decided it would be great fun to catch a bird. The plan was to turn the box upside down with a string attached to a twig that was to hold up the front edge to allow a bird to walk under it.

We then gathered up breadcrumbs and laid them to make a trail to lure the birds into the trap.

We settled down by laying on our stomachs at a distance from the box and waited, and waited, until eventually along came a cocky little sparrow that was adequately confident, curious, and sufficiently hungry to chance it.

It began to strut along pecking at the trail, not in the slightest bit suspicious about what may be the reason for his good fortune or how his luck might change. This little bird carried on along the line full of determination, in an urgent endeavour to satisfy his hunger by filling his belly before the rest of the bird population arrived to displace him and take their share.

He carried on pecking along the line, right under the edge of the flap and onward into the box. I was greatly impressed with David's composure because he was obviously waiting until there would be no possible escape for this little creature.

I soon thought, *"Come on Dave. Enough is enough. Pull the string or we'll lose this birdy"* but nothing happened. I tried to attract his attention by very gently gesturing to him to pull but to no avail.

I was only then that I realised he had fallen asleep.

So, I picked up a stone that was nearby and tried to throw it at the stick but missed completely and instead struck Dave fair and square in the middle of his forehead.

Being quick to realize my mistake did at least give me the advantage of being a good yard or two ahead of the wounded lion, such that I did manage to retain the gap and keep running until his aggression had somewhat waned and I could then ward off most of what would have otherwise been very painfully bruising blows.

OK, so maybe it wasn't glorious sunshine or even warm on every day of the year as I am about to show.

One morning when I was about six or seven years old and woke up, peeked behind the curtains and to my absolute delight and amazement there before me was an enormous blanket of snow, that reached up to my bedroom windowsill.

The high wind had drifted the snow and piled it up against the back of the house to a height of about three metres, so that now you couldn't see out of the downstairs back windows..

As soon as Dad realised we were awake he got us boys together and told us to not to attempt to get out through any of the back doors, because if they were opened it would release an avalanche of snow with us buried below it. We would then need a St Bernard to track our scent and dig us out.

With access via the doors being denied, he needed a safe means of avoiding the snow literally intruding into our home. The shovel was in the garden shed out of reach which meant an alternative was needed and after some scrabbling around in the house looking for an alternative he opted for a tea tray. Without further ado he decided that his means of access to deal with the drift should be out of an upstairs bedroom window.

He opened the sash window and holding on to the tea tray leapt out and immediately disappeared up to his shoulders in the snow and in so doing lost his 'shovel.'

He was then forced to use his hands to dig his way to where the tray had landed and with this in hand was able to get to the shed where his garden shovel was.

It took some considerable time and effort to firstly dig to the shed with the improvised shovel, however once he had the correct tool it still took quite a time to free a path to the kitchen door so that us children could get into the garden to play in the snow.

Dad decided to leave the other door blocked because enough was enough and in any case he was frozen through to the bones. Once he got indoors he ran himself a hot bath and sat in it for ages before he managed to thaw out completely.

Because the roads were impassable, work was out of the question. Now with access to his workshop he was able to busy himself making some snowshoes so that he could clear another pathway without sinking up to his knees in snow. But once they were finished and ready for use, he busied himself clearing the remaining essential pathways.

He then joined us playing in the snow. Although the original thought was to build a snowman this obviously soon changed to throwing snowballs at each other, which you will not be surprised to hear I was not overly keen on, but David, Chris and Dad seemed to delight in having this cold wet stuff hit them on most parts of their person. Not surprisingly, David was giving as good as he got and managed a direct hit on the back of Chris's head.

Chris was not happy about the fact his baby brother had managed to score and reacted by throwing them quite forcefully and from close range, until inevitably one hit David clear in the face.

Obviously, David got really upset at this and did

actually cry, but typical of David, he soon wiped his eyes and suddenly went for Chris, leapt at him with such ferocity that he knocked him clean over and then started stuffing snow in his face for all he was worth.

David was so aggressive that Chris seemed unable to defend himself, and Dad had to lift him off by the seat of his pants and dangle him in the air until he cooled.

A five-year-old David against a ten-year-old Goliath – No match. Moral - irrespective of your size, you upset Dave at your peril.

I am unable to say if this was the same fall of snow, but our ages at the time suggests that it may have been. Due to the amount the council workmen had shovelled it off the road and most of the pathway and piled it up against the back of the pavement so that it was now up to the height of a person.

David and I were playing snowballs in the front garden and just bending down to make another, when suddenly and unexpectantly I was hauled up off my feet. With legs dangling and flapping around in mid-air. I looked up to see I was being forcibly carried in suspension up to the front door by a Policeman. He then rammed on the door repeatedly until Mum answered, to be confronted by a very belligerent officer of the law demanding permission to execute this wayward missile throwing hooligan who had just cause his helmet to be forcibly removed by a well-aimed snowball. Mum, just stood bemused, looked at him quizzically and said, *"you've got it completely wrong I think, there is absolutely no way it was him and moreover I'd be obliged if you'd release you grip on his ear and let his feet touch the ground once again. However, if you would care to hang on here for a while, whilst I go and find a more likely suspect, I'm sure we can clear this matter up without you damaging your lungs any further."*

Mum had by then had a lot of practice and could winkle out possible wrongdoers from their lairs and probable hidey holes, but it still took a good while to route through them all.

Eventually, Mum returned with a very tiny little boy clinging sheepishly to his mother. The policeman was taken aback by the size of the alleged culprit, he was surely thinking, how could such a tiny little mite produce enough force to dislodge my helmet. But obviously he was not as aware of David as we were.

Before the constable could regain his power of speech, David interjected with a whimpered, *"sorry, sorry, sorry,"* and reinforced this pleading of innocence by pointing at me adding *"it was an accident I was trying to hit him."* The bobby was still standing motionless with mouth wide open when Mum backed up David's plea by adding *"so to my mind that's case closed. Good day to you officer"* and smartly closed the door in his face before he could reply.

I imagine you are thinking Yea, right! I do not believe a word of that. Okay, I do have to admit to over narrating the story a little bit, alright, quite a bit, but I can assure you the basis of the story is almost fact. The main difference being that David deliberately threw the snowball. Dave had just produced his next snowball to lob at me when, because the wall of snow had been piled so high, the only part of the policemen in view was the helmet on his head. I was watching as David ran to within thirty centimetres of the officer and let fly with the snowball, landed a perfect target gold score.

Dave was immediately on his heals and had soon disappeared round the corner toward the coal shed, while I just stood there riveted.

The bobby soon recovered his headgear and came through our gateway with a look of considerable displeasure on his face and of course could only see one possible suspect. *"What did you do that for"* He hollered.

I was still totally dumbfounded by David's total stupidity and being aware even at this young age of the power of the law, stood there dumbstruck.

I remained gripped in terror and unable to utter a word while Mr. Plod rattled on the front door. Mum answered and was immediately taken aback to find her 'wouldn't say boo to a goose' little son supposedly in police custody. A quick explanation and a short discussion soon led to David being hauled out to face the music. The sorry, sorry, bit was true as was the 'bad aim' plea. After pondering this explanation for a bit the policeman grudgingly accepting the 'accident,' brushed the snow from his helmet, donned it and bid his farewell and with a bit of a chuckle strode down the path to carry on his beat.

As soon as we were alone together, I just had to confront David after with a; *"You lied. I saw you, you did it on purpose."* He responded with a threat to cause me serious injury not just for then but for life if I ever let on, so please, do not let him know you know.

Nevertheless, this incident did at least teach me one particularly important lesson, which was when David start running, – don't stay to debate, RUN! And I remembered that lesson and used it many, many times after.

Holidaymakers are somewhat like migratory birds, in that there are very few of them during the off-season period. This did at least mean that from September through to early June we were able to enjoy the seaside more or less to ourselves.

When we did go to the beach in the summer it was generally not to Great Yarmouth, in fact rarely did we choose there. However, once the throngs of happy people dwindled to a trickle, we were able to enjoy the amenities more freely ourselves.

Walking along the beach as a family was quite a regular occurrence which I think we all really enjoyed.

My recollection is that we often also did this in mid-winter all wrapped up against the cold. Among these reminders is one where, whilst out walking one winters day, it started to snow and soon got to be Blizzard like, causing us to abandon the day and head for home.

By the time we got to our car the beach had been transformed from a sea of canary yellow sand to one of pure white snow much resembling a glacier. That is quite a spectacle to see and remains in one's mind long past when you were a young child, as you can see.

Another day and again a time worth a mention was as usual an off season walk along the beach pretty close to the water's edge and us children for whatever reason started running.

David and I were trying to keep up with Chris. I do not know why but I was closer to the water's edge than the others and decided to run through the "puddle" in front of me.

Suddenly I disappeared out of sight because the 'puddle' turned out to be well over a metre deep.

It was an enormous shock I can tell you. Besides, it being deep I had stumbled and ended up totally submerged. It was a few seconds before I was able to get myself together, but when I bobbed back up gasping for air and coughing up foul sea water, I found everyone else howling with laughter.

For the life of me, standing there like a drowned rat, I could not see any humour in my misfortune at all, but that did not seem to bother the rest of the family at all, and they continued to laugh relentlessly.

Obviously, I was completely drenched through, and as I say it was early winter so understandably it was not long before I was shivering uncontrollably.

I was quickly stripped naked and both Chris and David had to donate some of their clothes, which were supplemented with dad's overcoat as a means of trying to get warmth back into my body whilst we rushed back to the car.

It is worth mentioning that cars in them days did not have heaters, so I had to endure the shivering for a while. Nevertheless, as soon as we got home it was a quick dunk in a hot bath to get my body temperature back up.

Once again, this frail little lad had survived yet another of life's misadventures.

I think that this is a good time to add that writing this is being made more difficult by the fact that I do not have easy access to brother Chris, him being that bit older he would have greater clarity to these incidents and been able to give me a great deal more input.

But being a resident of Jacksonville, Florida USA, Chris is not readily available to talk to. Besides which his interaction is further marred by two things. One, the time difference here to there. Breakfast there is teatime here.

The second and more serious problem being the far greater time difference between his long-outmoded communication system to that of the twenty first century. He remains fixed in an era were dipping a quill into ink, writing in Latin onto parchment, sealing it with wax and then handing it to a stage-coachman to deliver remains his preferred method of conversing.

He has never seen the need for electronic devices, save maybe TV, all of which hinders my progress considerably. I do have this worrying vision of completing this series of tales and then having it severely red-penned by him later. Nevertheless, let's move on we cannot wait for the next stagecoach to arrive with a revision of the news.

That said, I stand by my statement that everything I recall is totally true.

I have made previous mention to a car. Yes, we did have a car which was an incredible rare possession for anybody to have back in the late 1940's. I think this must have been one of the perks of owning a garage that, besides repairing, also sold cars.

With that established I can now expand my family event limitations beyond Great Yarmouth and the beach. If we wanted to go to the beach for a picnic in the summer, by having the car, we could avoid the bustle of Great Yarmouth. Dad would drive us out to beaches further afield and this was invariably California Sands. No not the USA one – by the time we got there it would be time to come home!!.

Or even Caister-on-Sea. Both have glorious sandy beaches and as you can see in the photo below, substantial sand dunes behind.

However, in those days there was nothing there other than this beautiful sand. No, coffee kiosks, no amusements and most often not even another soul for as far as the eye could see.

We would generally meet up with the Lampshire's there. They were family friends, a couple that had a boy and a girl a bit older than us, which was good and added to the enjoyment because us kids had company for activities and playing games too.

To keep us entertained, we organised and played all the normal sorts of family games like cricket and rounders, as well as kid's activities like making sandcastles and burying one another in the sand.

The Lampshires owned a greengrocery in Great Yarmouth very close to R&M Motors. I believe the garage maintained their small open backed lorry, which is how Dad and Mr. Lampshire got to know each other. They clicked straight away because we were all from London.

The lorry was their only form of transport and besides being the means by which they got to these far-flung beaches, was also used by Mr. Lampshire to get to market to buy his produce.

They often came over to our house in the evenings and once we had been packed off to bed, we would hear them laughing and generally having a fun time playing cards and board games. Both my parents were tea-total so the exuberance was not due to alcohol induced pleasure.

I think that Mr Lampshire's name was Lenny and is something I can remember probably because it sort of rhymes. But, unfortunately, I cannot now remember the names of their children or their mum. When they were over at our house we had good fun too, because although that bit older they played fairly with us by not hogging all the limelight during the games and activities.

We did spend quite a bit of time with them, and they seemed to come over to us every time because I do not ever recall going to their place at all.

I have a faint recollection they lived in the flat above the shop with a small yard down at the back of the shop, so probably not suitable as a kids play area, whereas we had absolutely acres of space.

That's dad on the left, mum next to him, Mrs Lampshire, David, me, Uhmm - can't remember her name, then Chris. You might notice in the photo that it is warm enough for the children to be in shorts whereas their parents are still fully clothed. Any photos you might come across of holidaymakers in the 40's and even the 50s and 60's shows them fully clothed even on blazing hot days. It was just not the thing to bear your body to strangers or even good friends!!

To add to the beach fun, Dad had at some time acquired an ex-air-sea rescue inflatable dinghy. The dinghy was made of rubber and was supposed to hold up to ten people, which of course meant it was very heavy. Even though it came in a canvas bag with handles on the sides it was still quite a struggle to manhandle to the beach. So much so that Dad soon made a sledge so that it could be dragged to the beach in preference to carrying it. Because the dinghy required the two men to haul it over the dunes, the rest of us had to carry the remaining stuff from the car to the beach and that was a long trek through the dunes to where we wanted to pitch ourselves.

This dinghy had a lifeline that went all the way round it, to which they attached a rope, the other end of which was tied to an old potato sack filled up with sand to act as an anchor. Without which I'm sure we would have been swept away and ended up in Scandinavia if we were lucky, or Greenland if not.

The photo shown here is of the Lampshire's and Chris enjoying bobbing about on the water on one of our excursion days.

As you can see it was a big dingey and as I recall it came with the original compressed air tank and that was used to inflate it. Dad then used to charge the tank using the garage air compressor. The dingey would not fit in the car so again the Lampshire lorry was used to transport it to the beach site.

Although I can recall the days we went 'sailing' I cannot now remember ever being in the dingey myself. It did bob up and down quite a bit so, probably I was too scared to even get in and try it.

It was not just to California Sands, Caister or the like that the car would take us. We did venture to other places further afield. Albeit, sometimes without the Lampshire's.

Among the alternatives were trips around, through or on the Norfolk Broads. I can recall one time when we were actually in a motorboat cruising along on the broads, and Mr. L was 'captain' and Dad must have been the photographer sitting up front.

I think he wanted to clean the camera lens or something so Mum gave him her handkerchief. When he had finished with it, he threw it back to Mum but the wind caught it and she missed the catch and it ended up in the water. To me this was an incredibly distressing event such that at first my bottom lip began to quiver but soon I could not hold it any longer and instead burst into an uncontrollable fit of tears. Seventy plus years later and I can remember this with such clarity.

What a wuss!

It just goes to goes to show, what should be a seeming insignificant event to most normal children, did in fact scar me for life. I've just started sobbing again so please excuse me while I reach for more tissues to wipe my eyes!!

You probably already know that The Norfolk Broads is a beautiful part of the country as is a major part of that county, with many little gems to find if one cares to look.

One such gem is the little village of Potter Heigham, which was just a tiny little hamlet way back then.

Set within the Broads it is a charming little place well worth a visit and occasionally the destination for one of our many family car rides and picnics.

My personal dread was to learn that was to be where we were heading, because to get there we had to cross the ancient humpback bridge shown in the photo.

David and Chris loved this journey because they would encourage Dad to drive over the hump so fast that we all left our seats and landed with a bump, which made our stomachs jump too. Not a sensation I was at all pleased with, but my brothers thought this was hilarious. I have to say though, on the return journey he would normally ignore the barracking and cross the bridge very sedately saying something like *"I don't want to be laying on the ground in my suit trying to fix a broken spring thank-you."*

Another bridge that still sticks in my memory and for which I had similar dread, was again somewhere in Norfolk but try as I may, I cannot now locate where. The main feature of this bridge was that it was made entirely of wooden planks. It was a lift bridge and it had chains on either edge which were used to raise and lower it so that boats could pass through. The chains also doubled up as railings to prevent pedestrians from falling in the river. I assume this was originally built by the farming community to move the farm animals and carts across to the other side.

This bridge was not a humpback type but instead had a dip in the middle. – What? Yes a dip. On either side of the approach was a notice that read "Maximum Total Load Two Ton".

The first time we arrived at this bridge dad did stop and ponder it for a while. Then said *"I don't think the car weighs as much as that. But to be on the safe side, you all jump out. I'll drive it over and you can walk across and meet me the other side"*, another of mum and dad's 'discussions' took place, with the result that we all got out. Dad then gingerly drove the car down the slope with the chains rattling and the boards creaking and groaning until he and the car were back up on the other side.

Mum then screamed at Chris because he decided to run across whilst David was being restrained by mum from following Chris and doing likewise.

She was left with the very daunting task of crossing this rickety bridge with me giving my usual highly melodramatic performance, David struggling to get free of mum's grip and Chris jumping up and down on the bridge to make the chains jangle.

Safe on the other side, Dad lost his cool, leapt out of the car and was on his way back to 'complete the transfer', he gruffly demanded that Chris *'Get in the car now.'* Then obviously still fuming from the previous spat, without any nonsense swept both David and I up in his arms, stormed back towards the car while mum continued to bawl at him for the stupidity of it all. Dad reacted by promising to drop David and I in the river if we didn't stop protesting because this was stressing our mother.

I quietened my protest to a whimper rather than chance a dunk, but David still struggling to be released, would have been happy to go for a swim!

Other than that, the rest of the day went smoothly, and a good time was had by all, even though I cannot now recall whether the grass on the other side was greener or not.

You would be forgiven in wondering how could I possibly remember all these incidences from my early childhood? All I can say is many started as just a slight recollection in my mind, but as soon as I reminded other family members we were able to piece it all together. Others did originate from Chris or David, although I have only had a slight recollection initially.

I'm sure you have had times when a glimmer of a past event pops into your mind and you say to someone *"Do you remember the time that we ...."* and a discussion takes place with everyone chipping in their sixpeneth' to the story.

My Mum was great at recalling past events and could generally relay these with a lot of humour. Her stories were plentiful although I do have to say there are still very, very, many unanswered questions that we never thought to ask.

Like, what was the main reason for Dad giving up the garage. But so be it, that is how it is, and we cannot now dwell on what we do not and never will now know, because we did not think to ask.

Sorry, but I thought it a good time to make that clear right now, because a number of other equally true but seemingly 'tall stories' are about to unfold.

The next of these alleged 'tall stories' is again related to the car and a time when Dad seemed to have a perpetual hankering to find out what lies round the next corner.

This day we were again in Norfolk, no surprises there then, and driving close to the coast, when Dad decided to take what seemed like nothing more than a farm track for no other apparent reason than to see where it went, not that mum was that keen.

Everything was fine for a while, with the sea to our left, we were still reasonably close to the beach, so all was safe and relaxing or at least it appeared so. After a while, the track started to rise, and it was not long before we were above a cliff but still a good safe distance from the edge, but close enough to still enjoy the view. But as we moved further on the shrubbery and trees began to close in on the track and completely obscure the sea view.

There was now a barbed-wire fence to our right which was obviously a left over from war defences.

Mum then said *"Don't you think this is far enough Chris."*

Dad's reply was something like *"Don't panic it's a farm track so we are either going to end up at a farm or back on to another road"* so he carried on.

After travelling quite a bit further with no improvement to the track side restrictions, we followed round a curve to be suddenly confronted by a wartime defence pillbox, which was very deserted, abandoned and now totally blocking our path.

The track was too narrow to turn round at that point so Dad opened the door to get out and see if there was a way round it, and promptly slammed it. He was quiet for a bit then he said, *"Have you noticed the red triangles attached to the fence,"* adding *"that means we're very blooming close to a mine field"* or words to that effect.

A 'discussion' then takes place as mum points out she was not very happy about this drive from the outset. When things calmed down a bit, it is decided that the only answer is to reverse back from whence we came. If you know anything about 1940's cars, you will know that one of the omitted selling points was wing mirrors, but that was probably due to their lack of availability rather than indifferent salesmanship..

The car did have an internal rear-view mirror, but it was as good as useless because of the porthole size and position of the back window. With front windows wound down on both sides, Dad and Mum were forced to each look backward down the side of the car to ensure the car stayed in the tracks they came from. Clearly, they had to travel at snail's pace and needed to do this for some considerable distance.

At some point Mum, says *"There is another barbed wire fence hidden in the bushes on my side and that has little red triangle signs on it too."* Now we are moving even slower and even more cautious. It was somewhere about this point when Chris thinks he should do the decent thing and let his two younger siblings know that they are about to be blown to smithereens. With the result that the wimp goes into total meltdown, which is not exactly beneficial to careful control when navigating out of a minefield.

We now have two children bawling, me just because, well that's what I do, and Chris in response to the clout a severely stressed Mum had quite rightfully just given him. Whereas David thinks it all exciting and is loving every moment of his last few moments on this planet. It's about this point that Mum notices another pillbox hidden in the trees on her side.

Dad says *"its bound to have a clear track up to it, so I should be able to turn the car round there."* To say Mum was not happy with this is very much an understatement.

Dad then tried to explain that he was becoming increasingly worried because he was having to slip the clutch constantly and this together with the continuous driving in reverse gear were not beneficial to the longevity of the mechanical system of a car of this era.

After further 'debate' Dad's view prevailed and Mum and children were very cautiously alighted from the car and obliged to gingerly walk single file along the centre the tyre tracks we had previously driven down to a point that Mum considered was a safe distance.

With the family now safe Dad very carefully did what seemed like a ninety-nine-point turn to change direction and slowly came back to pick us up.

With the family now safely back in the car, dad followed the car tracks back to the main road at which point it was mum's turn to burst into tears in shear relief that her fears did not materialise.

Thereby, we lived to survive yet another day, despite one severely traumatised child fraying his parents' nerves and another now in one of his strops because he thought he had been very unfairly chastised for his jokey remark.

Some years later, when mum and I were recalling this she said on the way back, there was a very frosty atmosphere in the car and as we passed through a familiar village, to break the ice, Dad thought it would be a good idea to stop at the fish and chip shop he knew of around there. When we stopped Dad picked me up, gave my hair the usual ruffle, which was his normal demonstration of affection he used. *"Do you think we could all do with a big bag of chips."* he asked. We all answered with a resounding *"yes."*

I think he could see that I was still disturbed by the day's events and that he needed to lighten things up.

It is funny how the mind works, because I can clearly remember Dad sitting me on the top of the stainless-steel counter and picking David up and putting him beside me, whereas there are other parts of this tale that I had to rely upon my brothers to fill in the detail.

You may still be wondering if these happenings that I recall, are in fact true or just a figment of my imagination. That is for you to decide, whereas I can quite adamantly state that they are completely true, as is my next statement, but it is another you will probably be doubting the reality of.

I can categorically state that I have actually watched two aeroplanes crash in my life, one into the sea and the other on take-off. Fortunately, everybody survived.

The first was again when we were very young and involved a RAF Gloucester Meteor. I'm unsure where we were but I believe we were walking along the top of the sand dunes when we heard an aeroplane, the jet engine sounded in trouble. This made us look up to see if we could see it, suddenly Dad points and while I was still trying to spot it, shouts *"he's baled out!"* it was a long way off so initially I couldn't see the plane or the pilot, but when I spotted it, it was already in a nosedive and almost immediately plunged into the sea to made an almighty splash.

Despite Dad trying to direct me to the parachute coming down I could not see it, despite the pilot dangling below it.

It's another of those that if true, I would have thought, it would be a point of family discussion for years to come, but David does not remember seeing it, or it even being discussed, whereas Chris does, but his recollection differs from mine.

However, I'm sticking with my version because I have subsequently done a lot of research and found that quite a large number of Meteors have crashed into the North Sea at various times.

This research does nevertheless substantiate my claim in a number of ways. The picture I have always had in my mind totally corresponds to that of a Meteor. Of all the aviation incidents, as they are called, two crash sites are off Gt Yarmouth. One in 1951 and one in 1952. The plane in the May 1952 incident was some 13 miles out so it's unlikely we would have been able to see it ditch, whereas the 1st February 1951 crash description fits my minds-eye view of the incident perfectly and was only a couple of miles off shore.

The second aeroplane crash was in 1972 when I was just about thirty. A friend had invited me to watch a non-championship Formula One event called the Race of Champions at Brands Hatch. I cannot remember anything about the race whatsoever, other than food and drinks were mightily expensive and that Emerson Fittipaldi won the race.

Anyway, once the race had finished rather than spend hours trying to get out of the car park, we decided to leave if for an hour or so. Instead, we thought we would go to the venue airstrip and take photos of the various drivers getting into their aircraft and taking off. As the first driver came towards us, I grabbed my camera and was set up for my first shot, it was then that I realised that I had used every roll of film taking photos in the pits and while watching the race and to cap it all Terry had too.

Nevertheless, we were still in no hurry to leave and thought it would be good just to stay and watch anyway. A few of the drivers had their own aeroplanes and flew them themselves to and from races.

However, most of the non-driver pilots seemed to be part of the well to do elite that spent most of their time whiling away their days enjoying these expensive pastimes and showing us how life should be lived. Flying their plane to a motor race was seemingly a regular occurrence for them.

It looked like most race drivers were quite willing to pose for photos, so we were well disappointed that we had not saved some shots, but nevertheless were enjoying the spectacle of the take-offs along with many other. It was quite interesting because there didn't seem to be any sort of marshalling or order to the take-off, but there must have been because it all seemed to go like clockwork.

There was more excitement to come because every previous plane had taxied to the far end of the strip turned round to face into the wind before then opening up the throttles and taking off with a burst of speed.

This was until one bunch of about six exuberant people approached the airstrip in extremely joyous mood and staggering about quite a lot too. We looked at one another and thought I hope none of them are the pilot. After more childish jollity while getting into the plane they did eventually close the doors.

The pilot almost immediately started the engine and it seemed did not do any of the pre-flight checks all the others had, but just powered it up and pulled out from his stand halfway along the grass airstrip.

As soon as he had straightened onto the runway, he opened the throttles to full power.

We looked at each other and I said *"Surely he's not going to try and turn it round at that speed"* but I was wrong because he did.

He was not going to turn round at all and while we, together with the rest of the remaining crowd, stood dumfounded as we watched him attempt to take off instead. Like every other onlooker we held our breath because even to the untrained eye the plane did not seem to have sufficient speed to lift off, but take-off it did, just about.

However, the plane immediately started wavering about and to add more terror to this situation was going straight towards some big oak trees and they were not far away at all. The pilot even in his drunken state must have realised that if he carried on along his current trajectory, he would plough into the trees well before the top, so he tried to turn the plane to his left instead.

Like all of his decisions so far it was a disastrous one. The manoeuvre did indeed turn the plane sharp left, which made it stall unexpectedly, and it hung there stationery for short moment before turning on its left side and falling from the sky.

It was one of those moments where everything seems to be happening in slow motion. The left wing hit the ground first, crumpled and bent in two. I can still recall the crunching sound as the wing took most of the force which absorbed the shock before the plane miraculously landed on it wheels the right way up, and to my mind saved everyone inside the plane.

Within seconds the until then invisible marshals suddenly appeared from seemingly nowhere with fire extinguishers and fearing a fireball, started spraying foam directly onto the plane. Meanwhile, two others in fireproof suits very bravely ripped open the doors, and all the now shocked to sober occupants spilled out like a shot from a gun without the help of the marshals and sprinted to what they considered a safe distance, before collapsing in heaps. The race circuit fire engine arrived very soon after as did many policemen and we were then ordered to move away and go home because there was nothing to see. The fire engine then took over the foam spraying of the plane, which by the way had crashed into the middle of the car park that only minutes before had been totally full of cars.

Fortunately, there were now only a small number of cars there, but one of them was mine. The police would not let us go to get it, because the plane was full of fuel and there was still a chance of a fireball.

As I recall, it was some hours before we were allowed to collect my car and drive home. While we were being unavoidably detained we went off in search of sustenance but by then all the track amenities had close and gone home. By the time we were able to leave we were very thirsty and starving hungry.

You have to know that this was early 1970's so roadside stops were a rarity in the evening and although there were service stations along most major routes, their purpose was to sell petrol and diesel, from tiny kiosks and that restricted the provision of food and drinks. We had to settle for some crisps and a coke or something like that until we got back to London.

Please excuse my diversion into my adult afterlife but that event needed to be coordinated with the other aeroplane incident.

After that let us stay safely in bygone days for a bit, but before I relay the next home episode that comes to mind, I need to set a bit more background.

I mentioned the 'field' at the back of the garden, although I did say it was in the main set out as an orchard.

However, I did neglect to say the whole area was shaped rather like a blunt ended triangle. In the far-left corner butting up to the advertising hording was a 'barn' like building. The other end of the hording butted up to a flintstone wall, the other side of which was the Butchers Shop.

The advertising hording comprised a wooden framework covered with aluminium sheets and was about five metres high and seventy metres long.

Obviously, we were unable to see over the hording into the street below. This was frustrating for us because directly across the road from the hording was the local fire station. We could hear the fire engines leave with the firemen sitting along each side mercilessly clanging the bell to ensure everyone could hear them. No blaring sirens in them days I'm afraid. Not being able to see them would be annoying for any little boy, and girl too maybe.

When they received a 'shout', if the engine and crew turned right and then left at the traffic lights and we happened to be in the back garden rather than the field and we ran at our super fastest we did stand a slight, and I mean slight, chance of getting a fleeting glance of them going past the front of the house.

If they turned left or even right and right again, much to our annoyance, we would not see them at all.

The continuous disappointment of failing to view our great heroes depart with due fanfare, off to save persons and property meant that we needed a solution and fast. To us initially this was a challenge not really any greater than scaling Everest which in the late 1940's nobody had yet managed to achieve.

All it was going to take was a few concept meetings, an approved design, some labour, appropriate material, hard graft and close management of the whole project.

Thus, we abandoned all that science stuff and set about bashing a blooming great whole in the structure big enough to see through. Sadly though, despite the levels of energy expended, while using a rock as the main tool, we were not able to penetrate the aluminium sheet that formed the facing of the hording. Mind you we did manage to make a sizeable dent in it, easily noticeable to a less than pleased father and the owners of the hording.

OK, so we were then banned from seeing through the hording, but nobody has said we could not see over it. As you can guess, neither our sand cave project or this viewing area project had been risk assessed to any great degree and certainly not with much regard to Health & Safety.

Would lessons have been learnt from the previous mission and applied to this next project, don't be silly, of course not.

It just so happened that that Dad was into another major undertaking which was well in progress. I cannot now remember whether it was the new tool shed, chicken run, or rabbit hutch project but, what this did meant was that there was now an abundance of highly usable resources immediately available to us and just by utilising our safe cracking expertise they were ours for the taking. Hence, using David's deft skills with an oxy-acetylene torch it took no more than seconds to cut through the padlock of the locked toolbox.

Yes, OK you are right, I'm not being exactly truthful - Again!!. David had given a quick glance at the substantial five lever padlock, and it did seem to him to be a bit too challenging for a five-year-old.

What he actually did was to merely prise off the hinges using a readily available garden spade, simples! What he greatly coveted, and his reward for this highly illegal breaking and entering job, was just to lay his hands upon a claw hammer.

As soon as it became clear to me that an unlawful act was about to take place, I thought it would be a good time to disassociate myself with this. It seemed like a good time to creep away, go indoors, find a pencil and paper and do a bit of drawing.

However, I was not too long before Dave was at my side enquiring as to why I had disappeared. *"Dad is not going to be pleased"* I said, *"Shut up scaredy cat and come and help right now."*

Even though I knew in my heart of hearts that this was not going to go well I nevertheless obeyed my master and reluctantly followed along sheepishly and with the usual trepidation. We arrived at the site of his new assignment which was to make a scaling ladder to reach the top of the hording.

He had found the boxes of nails from Dad's job, selected many of the biggest and had already attempted to nail them into the sides of the angled wooden braces of the hording.

However, wielding a claw hammer one handed while holding nails with the other was proving to be a much more difficult task than his skills with a garden spade. His puny frame impeded his efforts at accurately striking the head of the nails. This meant he had managed to bend more than he had driven in.

To overcome this, his plan was that he needed a second person. What he now wanted was for me to hold the nail while he used both hands to wield the hammer. You can see where this is going, can't you!

Of course, I obliged – well a hammer can inflict a lot of damage on a person that refuses to comply with a simple request.

Hence, with shaking hand I held the nail, while he took an almighty swing with the hammer and missed, but only partially because he did manage to hit my wrist. He was a mile away from the intended target so obviously, a great deal more practice was going to be required.

Whilst I writhed on the floor in pain, or feigned pain to his mind, he said we should try again and this time I should try not to shake and just hold the nail still, that way he would be less likely to miss.

But I was resolute and made it abundantly clear that I was not going to just stand there while he broke every bone in my lower arm, so as usual I ran!

He was brandishing a pair of pliers when he found me again and politely asked me to return to assist, which I willingly did after noticing his determined look and that he still had the hammer in the other hand. Hence, I held the nails with the pliers while he swung the hammer with all his might. With more misses than hits and the pliers sent skywards even more often than that, he did get a few nails into the wood. Every nail that was firmly into the wood, was also bent, but still capable of supporting this five-year-old's weight.

It was about then that our absence had led Mum to suspect that all was not well. When she found us, she was quite rightly horrified at our project and even more so when she saw what had happened to the hinges of the toolbox and Dad's valuable nails. The net result was that we went to bed early on yet another of the many days we were in the doghouse.

A godsent in some respects because we were able to pretend to be fast asleep before Dad got home, so we managed to survive another round for that day.

OK, so Dad did catch up with us the next day, then severely reprimanded us for our vandalism, but not much was said about what we were trying to achieve. However, this is not the end of the story, because we still wanted to be able to see the fire engines leave the station. We found a reasonably long piece of rope and David had the idea that we might be able to throw it over one of the crossmembers of the hording supports closest to the barn.

He hoped that he would then be able to pull himself up and jump onto the roof of the barn. But try as we might, we could not do it.

I then had the idea that if we used a piece of the wood from Dad's project with the rope over the end we might just be able to get the end of it over the crossmember.

But each time we got the rope where we wanted it, as soon as we removed the wood, the rope would fall down. So, the idea was abandoned altogether for a while, until one day we could hear the fire station alarm bell ringing which meant any time soon the Fire tenders would soon leave the station.

At which point David does no more than use the few nailed in 'ladder rungs' then stretch up and straddle one of the angle struts, just like a Koala Bear does to go up a eucalyptus tree. He then inched his way up until he got to the cross strut and from there leapt to the roof of the barn.

He did miss seeing the first Fire engine but was up there in time to see the engine crewed by the retained firemen leave. He tried on this occasion and many times after to get me to try the same method of scaling to the top, but I just could not be coaxed into even attempting it, despite his heavy barracking and disbelief at my total failure to even attempt it. I am not sure how much later it would have been, but there did come a time when I could no longer bear his ever-persistent chiding coupled with the totally contemptuous attitude toward my frailties. So much so that I did eventually manage to convince myself to at least give it a try. Mind you, things had moved on and so the koala bear crawl method was no longer necessary.

By then Dad had made a very large wooden wheelbarrow which was generally stood up against the side of the barn. This meant that when positioned correctly, and with the aid of the previously abandoned rope, anybody with the agility of a monkey could spring up onto the top of the wooden body, then reach up, grab the rope to give himself purchase, and from there could then swing a leg onto the top of the wheelbarrow handle, grab the rope and with supreme effort body roll onto the roof of the barn.

However, for me it was made much easier because I then had an anchor man. After climbing onto the wheelbarrow, which I did manage to do unaided, Dave was there with the rope to help pull me up. OK, so I was now on the roof and should have been exhilarated and ecstatic at this achievement.

However, on this first occasion, because to the unexpected angle of the slope of the roof, I just lay there spread-eagled face down and remained terrified and totally unable to move a muscle for some time, until my "Instructor" took my hand and not too gently dragged me to the top.

So, there I was up there and able to gingerly peer over the top into the street below with my little brother by my side. That very quick look over led to an even quicker sit down due to me suffering a somewhat serious case of vertigo.

When I had been looking up at the top earlier it did not seem anyway near as high as the distance over the top did now, looking down.

My terror was not helped at all by the fact that now, sitting with legs astride the apex of the roof and gripping onto the hording for all I was worth, the garden seemed a heck of a long way down too.

Obviously, I hadn't considered this on the way up, otherwise he would never have been able to convince me to become a mountaineer.

I'm not sure how I managed to get down, but maybe the threat of a push helped. That said, I did venture up there quite often after that, so I must have overcome the dizzy feeling without medication somehow.

I do have to say that I did follow strict H&S guidelines throughout, albeit without the aid of hardhat and crash mat.

Whereas David as usual ignored the manual and just got bolder and bolder, so much so that he often sat on top of the hording with his feet dangling into the street. This did mean that when people passed by and noticed him, they would be horrified.

On one occasion, an elderly lady looked up and noticed him up there sitting astride the top and shouted up to him *"Get down right this minute before you fall"* David's response was to show even more bravado by standing up on the top and start walking along it like a tight rope walker. The top of the hording was probably twenty centimetres wide, but it was still a long way from the ground.

He says he did not see what her reaction was because he was busy watching his footing, but he is sure she must have been mortified because she stopped bawling at him.

Whereas I only ever just about poked my nose over the top, whilst gripping on to one of the cross struts for dear life, with the result that there was not much of me to see, so I rarely attracted any attention.

Because of the size and position of the hording and its relationship to our house, it was difficult for passers-by to identify where we had come from.

Unless of course you enquired at the butchers, he had early on formed the opinion that we were a couple of hooligans that were in need of a corrective thrashing.

His name was Mr. Drake and due to his willingness to tell tales we had classed him a proper snitch, nicknamed him *Drake-the-snake* and placed him at the top of our hit list.

Without the availability of telephones, *Drake the snake* would send his shop boy round to our house to tell Mum what we were up to, and she would arrive to find us up there once again and demand we get down right away. We would then give her a few minutes to leave before we climbed up there again. As you can see David very rarely thought about what the consequence of his actions might be and was very often surprised at people's reactions.

One prank during springtime, when the apples in the orchard were still very small, was to bash the boughs of the trees to get them to fall, then stuff our pockets full and run around throwing them at each other, Chris included.

Ok, if one hit you it hurt but it was unlikely to be a life-threatening blow, but it was fun, or at least Chris and David thought so, but I was not so keen.

Anyway, on one such occasion when fully armed we were on top of the barn and looking out for passers-by.

With only a nose showing, Dave was waiting for them and as soon as they passed, he would lob an apple at them and then duck down.

We would leave it a few seconds and then poke our heads up again to gain reaction. Generally, this meant people looking in all directions other than upward, so we did have a giggle watching these bemused people.

Until one day when David - I would never have had the nerve - threw one and he made a direct hit on the back of this chap's head.

He was quite a young man and as it turns out was an off-duty fireman from across the road, so he knew exactly where it had come from.

When we popped up for a look, he pointed at us and said, *"I know where you live."* We knew it was time to be back in the garden playing 'innocently' so we found another form of activity and were happily chasing one another, when a few minutes later mum was there, and we were, not for the first time in our short lives, frog marched unceremoniously to the front door to receive a lecture from the fireman. Actually, he didn't seem to be too annoyed, but just explained the consequences should we fall and also why we should be nice to people.

Mum said she just stood there in awe during the ticking-off because he was rather dishy. But there again, what's so surprising about that, I thought this is the main qualification for being a fireman.

If you are not bored to death with David's antics, here comes another one. You remember I said that he had developed a panache for climbing.

Well, in his early years his limitation was just his own physical height which restricted how far he could reach up without something to aid him.

All the antics described so far have not included climbing trees because he was not tall enough to reach even the lower boughs, even with the aid of the wheelbarrow.

Sometimes he was able to get to the lower branches, but it was his lack of height that was the limitation to him reaching any further and marred his ability to get to the upper boughs. One day he discovered a technique that enabled him to overcome the height obstacle and that was just quite simply to leap and grab. The day that happened he found he could do this to get to the next level and from there the next, and so on until in a short time was at the top. Just reaching up he had attempted many times but had been unable to progress very far, this new method just took courage.

This new art did mean leaping upward or even sideways to reach the next branch which he needed to do to perfection every time otherwise it would have had painful results. That was one of his amazing traits, he would try and try again, but once he got it, he got it and then became an expert instantly in everything he tried. Well physically that is – academically not so I'm afraid.

I have to say that the tree scaling was initially limited to Apple and Pear trees as they are generally not very tall, and the branches are comparatively close together.

However, plum and damson trees are another matter, and it took him all of two or three days into his newly acquired skill before he was able to scale to the terrifying height of one of those.

He would leap from branch to branch and be able to scramble up to the top of any tree in seconds. Whilst he was scaling apple trees I was generally able to watch and breathe almost naturally, however the bigger trees were another matter. I just could not watch, it was terrifying for me, so it was time to go and do a bit of drawing or reading and leave him to it.

Me in, with him out, was obviously soon noted by Mum and I would then have to go with her to find him. *"Come down at once"* became a regular call for a period after he had mastered this 'monkey' phase of his life. But all a waste of breath because moments after mum had left he'd be up there again, and again. I think mum gave up in the end and just thought she would simply bandage him up if he ever did fall. I for the life of me could not see the attraction with being at the top of a tree, or even halfway up it for that matter. To me it did not seem to serve any purpose in anybody's life except his. Until this point in our lives we had generally done everything together, however his newfound pleasure changed everything for a while. We had been forcibly separated by this newfound obsession of his, so for a while I was obliged to mope around in the garden, not daring to go indoors because mum would then have realised he was up to his antics again and would have been there in moments to order him down.

My activities co-ordinator would not then have

been too impressed, and I would again find myself trying to avoid sibling-imposed injury.

As I have intimated, he was very sure footed, but there was one occasion, when I was watching as he climbed a reasonably low apple tree, he stretched out grabbed a branch and as he went to pull himself up the branch snapped, and he came crashing down, striking other branches as he rapidly descended and then hit the ground flat on his back. He lay there stunned for a bit, with me leaning over him quite concerned and wondering if he had taken his last breath, then he suddenly sprung up, walked around rubbing his back and trying to compose himself although he did look in an awful lot of pain. This sudden and unexpected interruption to his monkey lessons lasted at least two minutes before he was clambering up again.

Actually, I lied again, he was out of action a lot longer than that. Even though he had fallen from a small apple tree. It was still quite a height and he must have hurt himself far greater than he was willing to let on. I cannot now remember how much he suffered if at all, but one thing is for certain it did not deter him from climbing for long, and once on the move again, it was not just limited to trees as you will hear later.

It would be better if I change tack now before you start getting bored, but a warning, there are still a number, well quite a number, of David capers to come.

Let's start with a bit of a geography lesson. Great Yarmouth is between Gorleston-on-Sea and Caister-on-Sea and situated on the coast about halfway down that semi-circular piece of land that juts out into the North Sea.

It was a fishing port for centuries before and for some time after we left, although I believe it is now mainly a service port for North Sea oil rigs.

The river Yare, runs from the mouth through the middle of the town, via the Norfolk Broads to Norwich. One side of the river mouth is Great Yarmouth, hence its name, and the other bank at the mouth is Gorleston-on-Sea.

If you were sailing into Great Yarmouth from the North Sea, the river mouth flows due west for about a hundred or so metres, then has a sharp ninety degree right turn to then flow north running parallel with the beach.

Now that you have your bearings I will continue. If Dad was working and we wanted to go to the beach it was generally Great Yarmouth that we went to. Although Gorleston was closer it was, well in the early days there anyway, still war fortified and very few amenities were actually open. Although Great Yarmouth beach was only about seven hundred metres due east of us, the river Yare was between us and the beach. We would often go by bus which took us over the bridge and into town. However, the bus dropped us off in the very popular area of the beach, which meant it was where the holiday makers preferred, so it was not favoured my mum. There was another route which Chris and David loved, and I hated with a passion, which was the ferry. This ferry was just a little rowing boat that held about ten people and was manned by one man who rowed it across. Among the many reasons I hated it was that the crossing point was still reasonably close to the harbour mouth, so the water would rise and fall in unison with the waves on the coast.

Even when you were trying to board the boat the river swell would make it rise and fall alarmingly. This added to the difficulty when boarding the ferry. For us kids the boatman would simply jump onto the bank and pick up us two smaller ones together, one in each arm, then as the boat rose, step smartly aboard and sit us down, same for Chris, but for Mum he'd stand in the middle of the boat hold her by the hand and say 'Now' when he wanted her to step aboard. Once we were seated he would row this tiny boat away while it bobbed up and down like a cork in a bathtub.

If that wasn't bad enough there was the constant flow of traffic along the river, a great deal of which totally dwarfed our little craft. Every passing ship produced even more swell to increase the discomfort. The ferryman had to stay constantly alert and could manoeuvre the boat on a sixpence so there should never have been any reason for my concerns.

The photo gives you an idea of how precarious the ferry was when loaded up with people and there's not a life vest in sight!

Looking at the photo, let me ask if you would cross from one side of the river to the other in a vessel that was sitting just a few centimetres above the water without so much as a life jacket to save you should the unexpected happen?

As you can imagine, due to the almost non-stop rowing the ferryman ended up built like an ox with arm muscles just like pop-eye. An attribute that held us all in good stead as you will hear later. Again, I imagine he must have ended up in the river at least once in his long career and was probably a good swimmer. Even then he surely could not have saved every passenger.

Although I do have to add that he was very jolly and would constantly try to make us laugh, which I am sure he did to take our minds, well mine at least, off the discomfort and fear.

Once on dry land and safe again we would still have a bit of a trek to get to the sea.

The section of the Denes directly in front of us at that time was still a military base although by then mainly used as a storage area for recovered military vehicles that had been shipped back from the war zone.

I can recall that looking over toward the base from the Gorleston side, there were these then redundant military vehicles spread for as far as the eye could see, the majority of which were in desert camouflage.

To be able to access the beach we had to pass Horatio Nelson's column and then needed to trek North parallel to the beach for a bit until we were passed the military base. At this point we would be really close to the Pleasure Beach which had a 'Scenic Railway' - an early form of roller-coaster - as its main attraction. It also had fairground rides and stalls selling hot-dogs, candyfloss, and the like.

I have a very faint recollection that there was a tunnel under the Scenic Railway that meant we could then get access to the beach. This was a god-sent because we would have by then walked about one and a half kilometres. The beach all along that part of the coast is covered in beautiful butter yellow sand, that when damp moulds easily into shapes that allowed us to have hours of fun making sandcastles, models. and pools.

I think it was on one of these rare height of summer visits, that we were making or had made some sandcastles and the three of us were ferrying buckets of water back and forth between the castles and the sea, which was only a few yards away.

Suddenly, Mum stands up saying, *"where's David? Why isn't he with you?"* I have to say this was less than a minute after Chris and I had arrived back with water.

Obviously, the instruction to all stay together had not fully sunk in, because we had clearly forgotten to bring him back from the water's edge with us.

Mum spent a few moments, with hands shielding her eyes from the bright sunshine, looking side to side along the seashore scanning for any sign of him through the throngs of visitors that descend during good days in summer.

She then screamed at us to stop playing and help her find him! People close by then realised Mums concerns and joined us in looking. As her fears heightened, mum asked the couple next to us to look after Chris and our things while she took me with her to look further afield.

Mum was calling his name throughout our search which soon attracted others to our plight, and this increased the number of eyes eager to find him.

It was then that one of them suggested that we went to the Red Cross hut which was not too far away. When we got there, we found that there was a very nice Red Cross man and lady manning it. They were there to deal with cuts, bruises, sand in the eyes and the like.

The man coaxed David's description from this now very traumatised mother and reassured her that this happens quite a lot every day and that they always manage to reunite every child with a mother.

Without mobile phones or walkie-talkies the man

had an alternative plan; "*See the green flag on the top of our hut, which now is at the bottom of the mast. Keep looking to see if it is at the top. If it is, then come back and see if you like the child we've found, if so take him, if not leave him with us and we'll drop him off at the orphanage on our way home.*"

This made Mum really laugh. In the meantime, we carried on scanning the beach and sea. I then asked what an orphanage was, and it took quite a bit of diplomacy and tact to explain it was all a joke and that he would be back with us all very soon.

All mum needed right then, whilst her nerves were severely frayed, was a another of her brood going into a frenzy and bawling at the top of his lungs, when all she needed just than was to study every inch of the beach and the sea to see if she could find her missing infant. I was told that in fact it was only a few minutes later that the flag went up and that the whole trauma was not more than half an hour long in total anyway. But for a fretting mother it all seemed like an eternity I'm sure. When we arrived, there was David totally unconcerned, still with his bucket and spade, and trying to make sandcastles right in front of the hut.

By recognising him Mum lost the once in a lifetime opportunity to relieve the family of the bane of our lives and I'm sure I would have got over losing my playmate eventually.

It seems that David had not seen us leave and then walked along the water's edge in the opposite direction to us, before realising he could not see us and just stood glancing around, displaying the aimless appearance of someone lost.

One lady realised he looked concerned, firstly

started to help him find us before eventually taking him to the Red Cross.

When we got back to Chris, Mum thanked the couple for minding him and our belongings and then despite our protests, quickly packed up everything and very soon we were prematurely on our way home by bus. For Mum that had been enough drama for today.

When we were talking about this many years later mum said that her heart was in her mouth from the outset because she wouldn't have put it past David to take his first swimming lesson uninstructed and try to swim to Holland as a starter.

As I have said before although I have a good recollection of many of these events, in a lot of cases I cannot now remember what age we were then, or in fact the order in which they happened.

What I can tell you is that these all occurred within a six-year period, from 1946 when we moved to Great Yarmouth and 1952 when we returned to the Greater London area again.

Chris was eight when we moved to the coast and was fourteen when we left, but I am not sure at what age he was when Mum started to take him with her to see movies at the Coliseum Cinema in Gorleston.

I do not remember mum having any real women friends, save for Mrs. Lampshire maybe, but as she lived the other side of town, cinema visits together were probably not feasible. These jaunts did at least get Mum out of the house for a bit.

I have to say that David and I did love these evenings with Dad because with him in charge anything could happen.

Dad was a qualified Mechanical Engineer, but also knowledgeable about Electrical as well as Chemical engineering, but I don't think he ever went on a Health and Safety course, in fact I not sure that such a thing existed then and even if it was available, he would have cried off. His thoughts were always that the evening should be educational. Although his primary thought was for us to learn a great deal from each evening, it was also meant to be immense fun for us children and I include him in the children remark.

Many of the "experiments," I am about to describe will make the parents and particularly mothers of the current and future generations hair curl and they will wonder why I would want to tell such young children about them.

But I plead that they are of the age now that we were when we physically carried many of them out under Dad's supervision. That said I appreciate that it is possible that these pages will be ripped from this book by those mums.

I must add all these experiments used items that were already in the kitchen or generally around the house or shed, so there was no need to buy anything in especially.

But before you all plead for me to reproduce them for you, I have to say that I am now very elderly, and I have forgotten what 'Ingredients' we would need! Is that what you Mums wanted to hear?

On with the first one then. At which point I have to give the statutory warning "KIDS DO NOT TRY THIS AT HOME"

This little "experiment" just required a tin can with a push on lid. Dad made a small whole in the bottom and the top of the can, we then filled the can with a secret ingredient from the kitchen, placed the can on the unlit gas stove, lid down, can upward, then held a lighted match over the hole in the top of the can to light it up like a candle.

After a number of seconds there would be an almighty bang and the can would fly in the air and hit the ceiling. We did do this in the garden one day, in fact it might have been the first time, but one of the neighbours banged on the front door thinking there had been an explosion, so we then had to made smaller versions indoors.

To ensure that I hold your interest, I'll drip feed the other "experiments" one at a time in between narrating other events.

I now tell you about the time my father tried his hardest to kill me and it was not one of the experiments. To be absolutely clear here, he did not try to do it with purpose it was totally accidental.

As I said earlier Health and Safety had not been dreamed of in those days, let alone put into practice. So, there was Dad busily constructing one of his many projects, this one being his new workshop and substantially improved tool 'vault'. In this wooden building he proposed to install benches and machinery to assist with the other projects, and a 'strong room' to deny his wayward son's any access to his precious tools.

The whole scheme was well advanced, and he was installing the rafters for the roof. At one point I very stupidly decided to walk directly below one that he was busy sawing to the correct length, with the obvious result that as the offcut fell end on, it hit me like a piledriver, fair and square on the top of the head and I went down like a ton of bricks. It knocked me out cold and I just lay there motionless.

Dad was back on the ground beside me in a split second. Supposedly I was oozing a lot of blood and mum, who was only feet away at the time and saw it all, was absolutely distraught at this sight and wanted to run and get an ambulance, but Dad stayed calm and dealt with the mishap. I was told, he picked me up just as I came too, and of course I made a bit of noise, well quite a bit of noise actually.

Dad retained his composure and just held my head under the cold water tap in the kitchen, with Mum still pleading to go for help. Apparently, he said something like *"Let's just bandage his head up and see how he is in half an hour."* Thus, with a wad of gauze covered in disinfectant cream held in place by yards and yard of bandage, I was told to sit quiet and see how it goes. Although I cannot remember much more about it now, I do have a recollection of having an enormous headache and feeling extremely sorry for myself.

Mum always said that she remained terrified for all that day and the next, thinking that I may have had more serious injuries and sat with me for the rest of the day and when I finally fell asleep was not even sure if I was in a coma or not. But hey I'm still here.

After reading through the last 'incident' I thought for the younger readers and there again, for most of their parents too, it would be a good time to give some more background on how practical matters were for ordinary folk during and just after the war.

The trigger thought here was, why didn't my Mum phone for an ambulance? Well, telephones were sited in tiny little red telephone boxes all owned by the General Post Office (GPO) and sited in totally obscure places and to be quite honest there were not very many of them anyway. I am sure it would have been difficult remembering where they all were when you were in panic mode. You could call 999 to summon an ambulance but it was such a nerve-racking experience people tended avoided calling one.

On another of our educational evenings with Dad, while Mum was at the cinema with Chris, we set about building a conveyor system. Dad must have spent a lot of time preparing this one by collecting lots of bits and pieces from his workshop and using them as components for the conveyor system. There was string, pulleys, bins made from empty tin cans, hooks and lots of other bits including marbles from our toy boxes. The set up was largely supported by the hooks and brackets that Dad had made in the workshop. It was all hung from the picture rail that went all round the room. It took quite a bit of time to set up, but once in place we could start.

Once the system was installed, we put the marbles into each low-level can, wind a crank and that wound a string vertically up and this lifted the series of cans.

At the top of the lift the bin turned over and the marbles fell out into another bin which was attached to a sloping set of guide strings. The weight of the marbles made the conveyor move by gravity and the bins went round the room before each one hit the unloader to tilt the bin and empty the marbles into a shoot that dropped them into a bucket.

Described here it may not sound very exciting, but at the time it was totally enthralling for us to see. This is well before YouTube where you can view similar "projects" these days.

On another cinema evening Dad got us to roll sheets of paper round a rod and glue them to make small paper tubes a bit smaller than Smartie tubes, but Dad would not tell us what they were for.

The next Mum night out he got us to watch while he mixed some secret "ingredients" together, then put this mixture into the tubes and at various times during filling we had to put very small amounts of various other extras in. When we had finished it was time for bed, but he would not tell us what we had just made.

This was probably sometime in late October, but I have no idea what year. A day or so later a parcel arrived from London which excited us, but again we were not allowed to open it or know what it was.

I can remember that it was nearly 5th November and we had gathered together lots of wood and dead bits off of the trees and built these into an enormous heap to make a bonfire.

When Guy Fawkes Day came Dad started the bonfire and it was not long before it was roaring with flames that reached well up into the sky and we soon became very excited by the blaze from this fire display.

It was then that the secret tubes were bought out and carefully set up along the side wall. Dad then used a taper to light the top of each tube in turn and it was then that we realised that what we had been making was fireworks. We had not seen fireworks before, so this was an entirely new experience for us.

What with the fireworks and the bonfire, we were having a great time enjoying ourselves. Then out came the box from London that had been sent by Nanny, Grandad, and Auntie Julie and this turned out to be even more fireworks. These included skyrockets, Catherine wheels, roman candles and even bangers, so the evening got even better and was made more special because Mum arrived with mugs of hot soup and snacks for us to devour while we watched.

I do have to add though that our own homemade fireworks were not at all anywhere near as good as the London ones.

They did not all work and even though those that did make a display similar to roman candles and volcanos they were rather overshadowed by the factory made ones. Nevertheless, we had great fun making them and were incredibly exhilarated by our achievement, even though in truth it was Dad that was actually the "chemist" and pyrotechnic operative.

David and I did actually make more fireworks when we were somewhat older, but under Dad's close supervision. When we told one of our friends that we were making our own, his eldest brother was absolutely appalled and made his displeasure known and threatened to call the police. I'm not sure whether it was illegal then, but one thing is for certain is that although some of the elements required were in most kitchen cabinets, we had to buy each of the remaining items each from a different chemists' shop to ensure they did not suspect what we wanted the product for.

I'm absolutely sure that making your own fireworks must be totally illegal these days, so again DO NOT TRY THIS AT HOME.

While we remain on this subject, Dad liked to tell the story that he and his father made fireworks for Guy Fawkes Day a number of times and each year they got a bit better at it. They used to prepare these in the covered sideway to the side of their house. However, one time while Dad was mixing the ingredients, he compressed the substance far too much and the whole mass of chemicals ignited in one great big flash.

Apparently, he was incredibly lucky in that although he burnt his hands, singed his hair and lost both his eyebrows he was otherwise unharmed by the detonation. However, although his Mum was obviously mightily relieved in that her one and only beloved son had not suffered any greater or lasting injury, she was most displeased and in fact highly annoyed that the explosion had scorched all the clothes that had been hanging there to dry, as well as blacken the walls in the covered way.

It seems that his father had not been there to supervise this time. Dad had become fed up with making lots of tiny batches, so he thought that for convenience and efficiency it would be better to make a larger batch whilst totally ignoring the possible consequences.

Many of the evening projects we experimented with back when we were very young are now shown on YouTube in abundance.

One of our favourites was making our own batteries with just ordinary bits and pieces Dad had in the shed and Mum had in the kitchen.

Essentially all you need is an electrolyte an anode and a cathode as the basic components. In other words, some sort of acidy liquid with two different conductors immersed in it. We tried quite a number of different combinations, because the aim was to make a torch light bulb shine. Of course, it would have been easier with a LED instead of the torch bulb because the LED would have needed a lot less current. But they simply had not yet been invented!

I think we tried salt, vinegar, kitchen soda and lots of other such kitchen products to produce the electrolyte, some were of no use at all, and others were really good. For the anode and cathode electrodes, we tried a variety of metals including steel, brass, copper, aluminium, zinc and lead.

I can remember that we were both highly enthused with the battery experiment initially, but due to the large combination of experiments it took quite a while to try them all, so we ended up losing a bit of interest.

But after we were nicely tucked up in bed, Dad set too and came up with a result, so that next time we got together he could show us which combination of items were needed to get the bulb to light to a satisfactory level.

On another one of these educational evenings, we had to take a candle, light it then use the melting wax to stick it down to hold it in place on a tin lid or saucer.

We then put it into a bowl and poured about five cm water round it, then lit the candle, placed an upside-down glass milk bottle over the candle and waited. Initially the water in the bottle was below that in the bowl but as oxygen was used up the water rose up until it was higher than the water level in the bowl.

Another on a similar vein involved dad putting small amount of water into an otherwise empty baked bean type can then soldering the lid closed. He then made a very small hole in the lid only.

He then placed the can onto the gas stove with a very low light under it. When steam began to come out of the hole in the lid, he turned off the gas and then quickly stuck some putty, or plasticine over the hole.

We then waited until suddenly the can completely collapsed as if it had been jumped on.

This experiment was designed to show us that the pressure of the air all around us all the time is sufficient to exert considerable force upon objects if you can create a pressure difference. By using steam to force the air out and then letting the steam condense back to water creates a vacuum causing the outside air pressure to crush the can.

There were experiments with putting a kettle of water on the stove and trying to hold down the lid with different weights. These combined experiments led to him making a 'cannon' which comprised a piece of metal tube about the size of a drinking straw plugged at one end. We had to put just a tiny drop of water down the 'barrel' then a roll a bit of cotton wool into a very tight ball like a cotton bud and plug it into the open end of the tube. We then had to place the 'cannon' over a lit night light type candle and wait and very soon the steam pressure would fire the cotton wool bud out with such force that the distance it travelled would totally amaze us.

There were other experiments like:

Making a zoetrope, which is an early method of being able to show images like horses apparently galloping or in our case matchstick men running. This required drawing a series of matchstick men with each image slightly different to the previous. These were than glued to a drum that had a number of slots (Windows) cut into it. The drum was then spun and if you looked through the slots the matchstick men appeared to be running.

I think I should say that if you do try any of the experiments I have described at home, everyone including the grown-ups needs googles and other appropriate protective equipment.

Putting a teaspoon of baking powder into various liquids such as vinegar, lemonade, cola and the like and then watch the reaction. The vinegar usually caused an extreme reaction and rapidly make a vast volume of foam. That one got a bit messy at times though.

The lemonade and similar products could be made to be extra gassy by adding just a minute amount of baking powder. Anything greater than that and it foamed up so much that it went all over the table, continued to bubble nicely and we would end up with very little left in the mixing container.

Another of our evening pastimes with dad was casting models.

We needed a cardboard box, some plaster of Paris (but in our case builder's thistle plaster), grease proof paper, heavy oil or grease, a few pieces of rod and one of the ornaments off the mantel piece.

The rods were needed to space and balance the subject ornament at the appropriate height for moulding. These were glued into the base of the cardboard box and the previously oiled/greased ornament was placed lightly on top to suspend it. The plaster was then mixed and poured all around the ornament to a level exactly halfway up the shape of the ornament and left to dry.

Once the plaster had set the top face was greased and the grease proof paper was closely cut to the shape of the object and placed on top of the now solid plaster. A new mix of plaster was made and poured to cover the complete ornament. When dry the mould was removed from the box and the grease proof paper allowed the two halves to be split.

Once split the original ornament was removed and the cavity greased. Dad then drilled a hole in the mould to use as a filling hole. The two halves were then aligned, placed together and taped and/or tied to keep them together. Following which a fresh mix of plaster was made and poured to fill the cavity and the whole left to dry. Once the mould was opened we had a near perfect copy of the original which we then painted up.

Another of dad's entertaining experiments involved

half a dozen drinking glasses, a sheet of newspaper, water colour paint and a jug of water. The first thing we did was lay out the glasses into a circle with each glass touching the next, then fill the first, third and fifth with water and add a different colour of water paint to each. We then took one sheet of newspaper and tore it into five 150 mm squares and then folded it along one side a few times, then folded each one in half. We then dipped one end into each water filled glass and the other end into the dry glass. We did this all the way round the circle, such that each glass had two pieces of paper touching the bottom of the glass.

We then sat and waited, it was a very slow process, but eventually we could see the coloured water progressing up the paper and over into the next glass. Then every few moments a drip of water would fall into the dry glasses from each of the now fully wet paper folds. Being aware that this process was going to be slow dad had got us to place the glasses onto a tea tray at the start. He could then place them on the table in the dining room when it was time for us to go to bed.

When we got up in the morning the water levels in every glass were then even, and we had an assortment of colours something like; blue, green, yellow, orange, red, because the colours in the adjacent classes had mixed. Dad then explained that this phenomenon is called a capillary action, which is how the plants and trees suck the water from the soil via the roots and transfer it to the branches of even the tallest trees.

Another inspiration that kept us entertained was when we made a water wheel and an Archimedes screw out of cardboard which we glued together. Dad then made this model waterproof by adding a coating of shellac over everything.

It did take a couple of evenings to make because it needed a couple of spindles and pulleys to connect the parts together and pipes to direct the water flow. The whole arrangement was then mounted onto a wooden board to make it transportable. We then only needed a breakfast bowl to act as a pond and we were ready to go. Once completed we placed it on the draining board in the kitchen and dad attached the hose to the tap and turned the water on slowly. The water from the tap turned the water wheel, which via the pulleys drove the Archimedes screw. The water from the wheel went into the 'pond' and the screw pumped it out again into the kitchen sink. This model was produced to show us some of the methods used to convert power before the advent of machines like steam engines.

Although there were many other 'experiments' and not all in the evenings, I think I have explained enough to give you a flavour of the trouble Dad went to entertain his children.

I wonder if you will agree with me if I say that we probably thought of these experiments more as entertainment than anything remotely educational. Whereas for Dad, the amusement aspect was the necessary element that kept us fascinated by each subject, although his main aim was far more forward thinking. His goal being to provide us with sufficient scientific knowledge so that we ended up with the ability to think well outside the box as we progressed through life.

Did I mention that my grandparents on my father side were of European descent? My grandad was German, and my grandmother was Dutch.

I believe that they came to England to find work and then stayed. They were married in Germany, but all their children were born here.

That is, my Aunts, Lena, Julia and Anna, and finally my Dad Christian. My Mum's parents were very much British having all been raised in Holloway, London.

I thought it was important to make you aware of this because this meant there were finite cultural differences between my parents' families.

One of them I highlight here is, in England we celebrate Christmas day, whereas our European neighbours consider Christmas eve to be the time to start the celebration.

Thus, before my Mum & Dad were married his family always rejoiced European and my Mums British.

The bonus for us being that when we came along, we got the best of both worlds because we celebrated both. There was one subtle change in that the traditional European Christmas Eve Dinner was overridden to remain a UK style Christmas Day lunch.

We still had a heap of presents in the early Christmas eve with food, treats, games and other entertainments. Then much like most children today, in the very early hours, we would wake to find stockings by our beds and besides that even more presents after breakfast and then another day of food, games and entertainment.

Dad like me, and probably a high proportion of the population absolutely loved his Christmas's. He would not be available to us on Christmas eve at all, and we would be locked out while he was busy decorating the lounge.

The centre piece would be an enormous Christmas Tree that sat in the bay window and reached from floor to ceiling. There would be lights, tinsel, baubles, and packets of sweets on the tree and lights, garlands, streamers and tinsel all-round the rooms.

Whilst this may not seem particularly difficult today, you must remember that, especially during and for some considerable years after the war, almost everything was rationed. All the items for the decorating had to be hand made using the limited materials that were available.

Mum was particularly good at producing craft products and among the raw materials she utilised was old newspaper which she would carefully wash to remove the print then iron flat out to dry and to remove the creases. She would then stick a number of layers together with flour paste so that she ended up with a card like material, which she would then paint, fold and then cut into decorative shapes.

For the tree she also made paper mâché figures like snowmen and fairies which she painted to make them look realistic. There were also leaves from the garden which she would paint as well as holly, and flower petals which she had picked and pressed when they were in season. So, the whole thing looked spectacular. Many of the decorations were extremely sensitive or had a short life, however those that could withstand handling after almost two weeks of hanging were then carefully dusted before packing away ready to be reused the following year.

The decorative lights in them days were very often glass models of lanterns, snowmen, Santa, fairies, and the like and all made of blown glass which made them extremely attractive but somewhat expensive, as well as sensitive. One little shake and the element would break and that would be the end of that bulb. Even with the greatest of care in packing them away some did not work next time.

This was made more difficult in that if just one bulb in the string was defunct none of the others would work either. The answer was to take a known good one and keep swapping it for each other one in the chain until the whole string lit up.

On one occasion after Dad tried this method, still the string did not light, which meant that this time more than one bulb in the string was dud.

Those complicated matters because it meant each bulb had to be removed in turn and tested individually.

Dad went off to get a tester that he had made, but I could not see why he needed the tester, so I thought I would help. I fitted one bulb to the spare holder instead and tried plugging the bulb and holder straight into a wall socket with the obvious result that there was a big flash and bang, all the lights went out and I ended up sitting on my backside startled and wondering why!

Circuit breakers were another future dream for humanity, which meant serious electrical overloads like I had just produced remained dependent upon a thin piece of copper wire called a fuse to disconnect the fault. After giving me a serious telling off, Dad had to then light a candle which was just about enough light to enable him to repair the blown fuse. Obviously putting a 12-volt bulb into a 240-volt socket is an action not to be recommended by anyone of any age!

As well as the adornments, the Christmas tree would also have many goodies attached to its branches. These included little packs of handmade sweets. What is remarkable about this is that sweets were considered a luxury and were totally banned from production during the war years. In fact, they only became available to buy again on 5th February 1953, some thirteen and a half years after the start of the war and eight years since it had finished!

Anyway, back to the story. Sugar itself was on ration, unless of course you serviced the van for a baker who used this product to add ridiculously small amounts as an 'essential' ingredient for his bread. Buying or exchanging goods off ration was a highly illegal practice that could get you a gaol sentence at the time.

I am not sure where the other ingredients came from but apparently Mum and Dad would make these unbelievably delicious sweets of varying types, including toffees and others that resembled jelly babies, coconut ice and dates filled with desiccated coconut, all wrapped up in little cellophane envelopes tied at each end with wool, Christmas cracker style. According to Mum she used to make about two hundred of these each year. We were limited to three a day each so that would be sufficient to last until twelfth night and just beyond.

I remember getting an absolute rocket from Mum and Dad because I saved some and gave them to the kids at school when we returned, and of course Miss B unwittingly thanked Mum and Dad for the gesture and this got me into trouble. The reason they were less than happy with my kind deed was that I was innocently spreading the knowledge that my parents had the wherewithal to procure ingredients that the other children's parents could not even dream of, and to add fuel to that fire, one of the benefiting children's father was a policeman!

Dad obviously had visions of serving time for my stupidity. I do have to say that unfortunately this was not the only occasion that I got my parents into a tight spot due to inadvertently 'dobbing them in' for their under the counter activity. But more of that later.

Dad having made friends with a baker had other advantages as did being the local butcher's neighbour. - Remember him – *Drake-the-snake* that would report our misdemeanours at the drop of a hat. It seems that when it came to making a quick buck his idea of morality had a different slant. You can see that 70 years later I'm still sore about it!!.

Anyway, Mum among her many attributes was a superb cook and could produce mince pies and sausage rolls to die for, and Dad knew who to chat with to broker an exchange for what would have otherwise been unavailable ingredients.

For many, many years after we had grown up mum used to spend all day Christmas Eve making an enormous batch of sausage rolls and mince pies. She would then divide than up so that all of her family had a batch to take home and devour at their pleasure. I still like to think back to the days between Christmas and New Year sitting there in the evenings watching the TV with a tot of whisky and a plate with at least half a dozen sausage rolls to eat. Such pleasure!

I have previously intimated that we had an abundance of presents for Christmas. However, this was not quite a matter of my parents popping into Gamleys and coming out with arms full of goodies.

Obviously, the war effort meant that making Spitfires, tanks, battleships, and the like, rightfully took precedence over making lookalike toy versions of these for children. In fact, children's toys of any type were again a no-no. This remained the situation for quite a few years after the war and when it was then just a distant memory.

Unless of course you had a dad that could make anything or at least recycle them. These included refurbishing another child's cast-offs or taking items that were seemingly scrap and turning them into a child's toy. One year we had brightly coloured 'new' bikes that had previously been scratched and battered by earlier beneficiaries and he lovingly stripped off all the old paint and renewed it with new. He even made replica rifles from wood and metal tube that really looked the business and actually shot corks. Chris received a naval harbour and full battleship fleet all handmade from wood and painted up in true warships colours. But the pièce de la resistance was the Jeep he made for us for Christmas 1948. The photo is from Easter 1949, so I was coming up to seven years old and David five. Outwardly the car was very much like a wartime version of the Jeeps you have seen in American war films and as you can see nothing like the Chelsea Tractor type Jeeps of today.

It was a pedal car, which meant that one of us had to sit in the front and peddle while the other rode in luxury in the back, it didn't have independent rear suspension, so to call it luxury is probably over-egging it just a bit.

This Jeep figures quite a bit throughout this book so I'll carry on with the Christmas theme for a bit and come back to it a few pages on.

As I said earlier, Christmas was almost as enjoyable for Dad as it was for us boys. TV was little more than just a concept at that time with exclusive BBC broadcasting rights providing only a couple of hours of programmes each day, however even for my garage owning entrepreneur father television was an out of reach dream.

Whereas BBC radio had been around since the 1920s and by the late 1940s provided three diverse radio stations.

Mum would have the radio on most of the day and would sing along with the songs of the day. She had a good singing voice and in fact was the singer for a band back in her youth.

Whereas I am unsure whether Dad liked the songs of the day or any ordinary songs for that matter, because I cannot remember him ever breaking into song, come to that, neither do I recall him ever listening to music or songs on the radio other than on Christmas Eve, when he would bring the radio into the lounge and tune into the BBC Light Programme so that he could listen to the Christmas carols which he said gave him the Christmas Spirit. Both Mum and Dad were tea-total, so they needed something else to lift them I suppose.

One Christmas Eve carol singers knocked on the door and Dad answered the door and instead of paying them off and shutting the door he immediately invited them in to get them to make his evening by singing his favourite carols. Many years later during one of our moments of recollection I asked him about this and the fact that he actually got one boy to sing Silent Night as a solo. He said that he realised that the boy had a good soprano voice and when he spoke to him, it turned out he sung in the church choir. Silent Night was Dads all-time favourite carol, but initially the boy was reluctant to sing it solo. The stakes were then raised until the offer was too good to refuse.

Dad was over the moon with this rendition of his much-loved Christmas carol.

With Dad then in full Christmas mode I am sure that besides this particular lad's windfall, he would have made sure the remaining singers were adequately compensated as well and probably fed until full to the brim with Christmas food and goodies too. Although I'm sure he would have enquired whether any of their parents or other relatives were employed by the constabulary or judiciary before distributing them.

As children what we failed to appreciate at the time was the sheer ingenuity that dad possessed which meant he would continually dream up new ways to entertain. One Christmas afternoon he surprised us all by setting up a white bed sheet in front of the Christmas tree, which had us all bemused. He then carted in an assortment of mechanical bits and pieces and started assembling these together. Once he had finished we were still unsure what it was. Chris then leapt up all excited because he had worked out it was a film projector, and we would soon be able to watch movies. I wasn't until it was fully assembled that David and I could agree with him.

The only way of watching movies during that era was at the cinema. Unless of course you had a dad that knew where to go to 'get the goods' you needed if you wanted to come up with these sorts of surprises to entertain his family. Remember that television was an infant invention far beyond the reach of normal mortals, but for those with mixed morals like butchers it was an affordable luxury! Entertainment devices and apps like Net-flix, Prime TV, tablets, smart phones and the like were not even a consideration for futuristic comics let alone scientist's minds.

Where the projector and film came from or where it went after I have no idea, but it was the real deal. The projector was a full 35mm version the same as cinema versions of the day. The film reels were about 450mm diameter so again that's something like the cinema size at the time.

Once Dad had managed to set it all up, the ceiling lights were switched off and we were excited to watch animated movies of Felix the Cat and Pop-eye the Sailor.

They were genuine movies, but the downside is they were not talkies, to compensate, captions would pop up at various points during the film. If you have ever watched reruns of silent movies, you will know what I mean.

Everything was going well, when suddenly the picture froze with Pop-eye standing there like a statue flexing those enormous biceps. Then without warning a small hole appeared in the middle of the picture, which rapidly enlarged until the whole screen was white. All of this occurred within a few short seconds and instantly we could smell smoke, which seemed to indicate all was not well.

Dad instantly pulled the plug and turned on the top light so that he could investigate. To be able to project the picture to a distant screen the projector lamps needed to be extremely powerful. Stalling the film meant the power was then concentrated on one frame of the film which melted the film. The film material was celluloid, a highly flammable material, that could have ignited and would have then been almost impossible to extinguish. The film is driven along by the perforations (the little square holes) in both edges, and it appears that at the point it stalled the perforations had been damaged so that they were not being moved by the sprocket. Realising the problem Dad cut out the damage section then re-joined (spliced) the film at the point of the cut.

He then ran the complete film forward with the lamp off to ensure there were no other damaged sections then backwards again to the beginning before again turning on the lamp and restarting the film.

It would have been nice if whilst all this was going on an usherette had offered us choc-ices to while away the time, but sadly they were also a totally (government banned) unavailable product at the time!!

Anyway, we were then able to watch Felix and Pop-eye without further incident.

It might amaze you to know, that these two films were the first that David and I had ever seen so we were absolutely enthralled and enlightened by the experience of watching pictures move across the screen.

Even though the whole concept had been explained a number of times such that we had a bit of an understanding, it was still difficult for us to completely envisage the moving images.

If you think about it the only possible way for us to have seen anything like it previously would have been to go to a cinema, which at the time was an experience we had yet to be given the opportunity to enjoy. Although, it could not have been long after this that Mum took me to see Song of the South with Uncle Rufus singing Zipity-Do-Da and again I was totally captivated. So, there you have it, the first ever talking movie that I saw was Song of the South a Disney partially animated film.

All of the films that Chris attended at the cinema with mum were either 'U' or 'A' classified which meant he was able to watch all Disney films and most Cowboy and War films that were produced.

We would sit with Chris the following day and listen while he told us about the film. We then relayed what dad had dreamed up for us to do while he was at the cinema.

Just to conclude this section, I have to say that I never thought to ask where the 'cinema' kit came from, because I do not recall it ever being used again.

Whether dad purchased it and after this viewing realised the dangers and sold it again, or whether he borrowed or hired it we will never know. But what is clear is that he never failed to come up with his own unique brand of family entertainment. I could add that this may have been his way of attempting to divert his brood away for their own very questionable methods of enjoying themselves.

Carrying on with the Christmas theme, and yes, I do agree it goes off in many directions at times before arriving back to where it left off, but there again it has been a job to make the whole thing flow smoothly into the next, so please bear with me some more.

Christmas lunch was very much the traditional one we expect today, less the turkey. But there again we generally had chicken and at least one year it was goose. I remember mum telling us that although she had cooked the goose along with the other food for the meal, as soon as dad started to carve the bird she burst into tears and rushed out of the room. She had left because she didn't want us children to realise the reason for her tears.

She had this vision of the goose gaily strutting his stuff the previous day and there she was about to devour it, so it suddenly bought a lump in her throat and tears to her eyes. It took her a few moments for her to compose herself before she strode back in sat down and had to force the first few slices down. She said the silly thing was that we had had many meals before with home produced meat and it had not had the same effect previously.

She added that it was probably that the previous day this cocky leader of the gaggle had been livelier than usual and strutted about made a lot of noise right up to the point he was handed to the butcher. And suddenly he went quiet.

My parents had, when all is said and done, raised our feathered brood as a means of providing food for the family either as meat or as exchange for other foodstuffs. The brokered negotiations with our close neighbourhood butcher *Drake the snake* avoided Dad the messy business of dressing these birds ready for Christmas or indeed any bird or rabbit at any other time of the year.

It might have been foul mouth Graham's Dad the greengrocer almost opposite the house and both our fathers having an arrangement to ensure his van remained reliable. It might even have been the Lampshires. Whichever it was, the arrangements ensured traditional vegetables were plentiful enough for a proper finish to a special Christmas Lunch.

This was followed by Mums own distinctive recipe homemade Christmas pudding, with whipped cream topping, what else would one have?

Remember Jacques, Chris's school friend? Well, his dad owned the dairy just along the road from us, but their milk deliveries were still by horse and cart, with some by bicycle, removing the possibility of the usual bartering method for a goods exchange.

However, a sweet smile from their sons very nice school friend Chris, was all that was needed to ensure the traditional Christmas pudding was indeed topped in the proper manner.

With Christmas behind us but while still talking food, a day worthy of mention but not really a great event as I recall, but who knows, maybe it was. It was the day Dad arrived home with two bakers' trays full of cakes.

The number of cakes would be far too many for us as a family to consume before they went stale. I do remember seeing the cream buns set in rows. They looked like bread rolls but sweet and were all diagonally cut through and the slit was filled with clotted cream. There were also little fairy cakes, made of squares of sponge cake and coated with different coloured icing and a jelly tot type sweet on the top of each.

I tend to think it must have been a birthday party for Chris, because by then he would have been in secondary school and it would have needed at least a whole class of kids to completely demolish the evidence of possibly yet another criminal conspiracy. There were far too many for the recipients to have been Mine and David's total school attendees.

Goodness knows how or where the baker got the ingredients from, because it is unlikely we would have had sufficient coupons to cover the number of cakes, so I am forced to say these must have been yet another furtive trading arrangement where the baker exchanged the fruits of his expertise with those of a motor mechanic.

I did mention, and in fact may have overstated, that we had many feathered friends the reasons for which I will now expand this a little further.

Throughout the rationing period one could produce food for their own purpose only, which meant that they must not sell it. Dad though it would be good to get some chickens as we would then have extra eggs to those allowed by the ration book which was 1 egg per person per week and these remained rationed until July 1954 that's nine years after the war finished.

Ok, enough of the history lesson. So, Dad went out to buy some chickens. Well, according to Mum it was not actually quite like that. He did go to Potter Higham market to buy chickens but when he realised the price of each chicken, he bought twelve fertile eggs instead.

The first problem was that they had to be kept warm for the drive back. He had taken a flask of tea with him to drink, but by the time he got to buying chick eggs he had drunk it all.

Not to be outdone he managed to get a market stall holder selling teas to fill his flask with supposedly hot, but by then just warm water. He then very carefully wrapped the flask in his jumper with eggs all round it and gingerly drove home. When Dad arrived home, we were overjoyed to see the eggs, but he had work to do, so after refilling the flask with warmer water placing it back in his jumper with the eggs, he was off to the workshop with us in tow.

We became more and more inquisitive to know what it was he was making, and soon learned it was to be an incubator. This was going to be a box made from plywood, the lid of which had a lamp holder and low wattage lamp fitted into it, to provide the heat that would keep the embryos warm until they hatched into chicks.

He then finished the box off with a few ventilation holes, a Perspex viewing window in the side and cotton wool in the bottom.

We were then allowed to take each egg from its temporary home and place it carefully into the box. Then with rising interest we switched on the light, then waited and sure enough the incubator heating system was soon up to breeding temperature.

We found it tough waiting the three weeks it takes to hatch, which seems like a lifetime when you are young. I think only eight of the eggs eventually hatched but unfortunately one of them died overnight, which upset us greatly at the time. In fact, only four actually grew up to become chickens and one of them was a cock so only three hens to provide us with eggs.

Dad was greatly enthused by the success of the 'transport' version incubator and was soon off to buy more chicks such that eventually we had something like twenty free range egg producing hens wandering around the field. Dad then made straw lined coops for them to go to lay their eggs, despite this luxury comfort for laying, we would quite often find the odd egg was laid in a remote place in the field.

Then an unthinkable disaster struck, Dad went to the field one morning but was back very soon after to tell mum not to let us out to play under any circumstances.

He had arrived at the field only to find that a fox had been there in the night and had killed a great number of the chickens.

That is the thing about foxes, they kill just for the pleasure of slaughtering every animal that cannot fight back or get away.

Anyway, a very emotional Dad then had to dig a pit and bury all the carcasses to a depth that would be too great for the fox to exhume them.

He then set about constructing a large fully enclosed wire netting sided chicken run, complete with sleeping hutches and egg laying pens, and then restocked. The chickens were free range during the day and returned to the run before dark, before the nocturnal fox went out hunting again. To Dad's amazement he found that the fox had burrowed under the run during another night, however he could account for every chicken so thought the fox may have been disturbed or had decided to rest and come back the next night.

With the chickens in the field that day Dad dug down about thirty cm lay wire netting flat down all over the floor of the run and then attach this to the wall netting, so that the chickens were then cocooned in the run. He then had to replace all the earth back, so that the chickens could still scratch and peck around as usual. I still have this thought of the fox uttered a few expletives when he arrived that evening only to find all his burrowing had led to nothing more than an unattainable dream for the taste and aroma of chicken burger!!

Do you remember I mentioned that a cockerel was one of the first hatched, well if it was the same one, he grew up to be massive as chickens go, and protected his ladies valiantly. If his hareem were pecking around in the field he would be quite comfortable, provided that you did not move too fast when in his or the hen's vicinity. However, he was totally different inside the run, which was his domain and where he was the undisputed ruler.

Just entering the run meant he would go into a frenzy, leap up and down on the spot with wings flapping furiously, and this would cause the hens to do a more subdued version of the same. Move any closer to him or a hen and he would go into full war mode, with talons fully exposed he would fly at your head, which you can imagine was a very frightening and effective tactic, because you had no alternative but to retreat or be injured.

There were only two people that could enter the run, Dad and David. Dad did tell us that he took no notice of the war dance until the day he went to pick up one of the hens and the cockerel went into full fighting mode. Dad was bending down at the time and the cock landed on his head and was pecking at his scalp for all he was worth. I imagine more in surprise than panic that Dad reacted and managed to grab the cockerel's neck to stop him pecking and was then able to fold in the cock's wings and tuck him under his arm.

Obviously, even with a hand round his neck and the forcibly folded wings both restricting its fighting power, the cock continued to attempt a fight, but with all his armament disabled, he did eventually give up and become almost passive again which gave Dad the opportunity to open the door and throw him outside, where he just strutted up and down voicing his irritation.

It seems Dad had demonstrated who was supreme master of this particular chicken run, so from that day on all the cockerel did was to swagger round the run and assert vocal discontent each time Dad entered his former domain but was never eager to duel again.

David also mastered this feathered fiend, but I think this was out of mutual admiration and probably born from his love of all our menagerie. Each of which David would have cuddled up to from the moment of their arrival, and I suppose the cockerel just regarded him as 'family'. Whereas I never was one for picking up the animals, especially ones with claws, beaks, or teeth. The exception being when they were very tiny, like newly born chicks, so it is not surprising that I did not naturally bond with any of them. In fact, although I like some animals, like dogs for instance, I have never felt the need to own one or become emotionally attached with one to any great degree.

Returning to current topic, when David entered the run the cock would vocally acknowledge his entry but strangely there never seemed to be any likelihood of an attack.

Notwithstanding, had that occurred I am absolutely certain the loser would have ended up just a few feathers short of oven ready!

I had earlier said "I mentioned that we had many feathered friends" and a couple of pages later I have only mentioned chickens. Well, history shows that Dad got somewhat addicted to Potter Higham market, because over a period of time we ended up with ducks, geese and rabbits in addition to the Chickens. I am not now sure whether the additional fowls had separate enclosed runs but feel they must have because I believe there was only ever the one fox incident. I think the additional fowl were above chick age when we added them to the animal stock.

This was probably because rearing a brood from eggs took a great deal of close care, and even with this duty and devotion, a significant proportion of every brood either did not hatch or died before maturity, leaving an unwanted heart wrenching feeling of loss, as well as despair at the sheer brutality of nature.

When it came to 'family protection' the geese are a noisy breed of bird. They seem to have this need to warn you not to come any closer even when you are quite a distance away and not moving in their direction anyway. Once one starts, they all join in and if the deafening level doesn't make you back off then the goose certainly will when he rushes in and rapidly pecks at you with the speed of a woodpecker, and it hurts I can tell you. I obviously avoided them like the plague rather than endure the force of its displeasure.

David once again could stride right through their gaggle and if the goose did object, he would just walk slowly towards it, and although the goose would make its displeasure known quite forcefully, these were just idle threats, since the goose would keep his eye on him but back off, with Dave staring him out as he moved forward and past them.

Right from the beginning the chickens had to be fed with 'mash' a government-controlled product that had a separate rationing system. The mash was needed in addition to the feed to supplement what chickens scratched from the ground and by eating grass and weeds.

The mash was supposed to encourage egg laying and to ensure the eggs contained a high nutrition content.

This mixture was boiled up together with other ingredients like the left-over potato peelings, outer cabbage leaves and the like. In the unlikely event there was ever any leftover food or bread, not that there ever was, then that went in too. The mix was then too wet for the chickens so after straining off most of the water Dad used to add sawdust that he got from the sweepings off the butcher's floor. Way back then it was very common for all butcher's shop floors to be sprinkled with a new covering of sawdust first thing every morning.

This had a practical use in that if pieces of meat and the like did fall on the floor it could easily be swept to one side and a new sprinkle of sawdust added, thereby the floor did not need to be mopped every time. It was then swept up and binned every evening. By adding this to the mash, I half expected the eggs to have a wooden shell so that one needed a saw to open them.

As the number of fowl increased so did the amount of feed required and eventually, we ended up with a container sufficiently large for a single batch mix.

I'm not sure how dad managed to fit it in between running the garage and all the other household and 'farming' jobs that he was responsible for but, it seemed to be Dad's job when it came to feeding the chickens, ducks and geese.

There were times when we would be relegated to carry out this essential function, which I hated with a passion, because the mix smelt foul. Anyway, the container was too heavy for us youngsters to carry so Mum used to lift it into our little wheelbarrow and off we would go to the field. Because this meant entering the run, I would adamantly refuse to feed them so generally David would ladle out the portions to each. He was quite happy if they decided to jump on his back or even his head in their enthusiasm to get at the food, it never seemed to bother him one little bit.

Although we rarely saw our London based relatives, Nanny Holland and Auntie Julie did come on holiday to visit us a couple of time whilst we were in Gt. Yarmouth. It was while they were holidaying with us on one occasion and for whatever reason Auntie Julie decided to feed the family 'birds."

So off she did trot with the container in hand, only to return not very soon after running for all she was worth and screaming at the top of her voice with the cockerel's claws holding him to the back of her coat while he rapidly pecked at her scalp.

Mum tried to intervene but was beaten back by the flapping wings, so ended up using the broom to force him into submission.

Not long after this he was returned to us by *Drake-the snake*, less the inedible bits, and a delicious meal he was too. For the hen's protector to be turned into food, Dad must have decided the need for any more fertilised eggs was over.

That leads me to the actual egg production and generally we did have eggs daily. Although these were predominantly chicken eggs we did have duck and geese eggs too from time to time.

Duck eggs are quite a bit larger than their chicken counterpart and the yolk is larger making the whole meal more nutritious. Geese eggs are about three times bigger than chicken eggs and again are more nutritious and make a fantastic family size omelette.

I mentioned earlier that eggs were still on ration throughout the time we were in Gt. Yarmouth and that to get the 'mash' you need to have a ration book. However, in exchange for receiving 'mash' people were expected to donate a proportion of their eggs. I imagine that Dad would have bought his 'mash' *under the counter* rather than having to give part of this commodity away.

His 'trading' activity was something Dad did 'mention' to me at some time and included an arrangement for our fowl and eggs with the butcher, baker, and leaving out the candle stick maker, but including Longs the dairy, Willis's the greengrocer and Wrag's the general grocer.

He also told of a wartime rations story when he was still in London, had come out of a friend's butcher's shop after a 'purchase' and upon looking both ways spotted a policeman not far away.

He stopped and got out a cigarette and then casually walked up to the bobby, put down his bag and asked the copper *"Have you got a light mate"* he did not give Dad's bag a second thought but just produced a box of matches and lit his cigarette. Dad thanked him and walked off feeling very relieved and with his heart rate slowing towards normal.

Now for another of my indiscretions. I am not sure who the lady was but my Mum and her were talking in the kitchen. I'm not sure what the context of the conversation was but eggs were mentioned, but while mum and the lady were chatting, I did no more that whip open the larder door and show the lady the tray of possibly twenty or so eggs standing there. Mum's face went white, and she glared at me so that I knew that maybe that I had not made my wisest ever decision. When the woman left, Mum ripped me off a right strip. Moral – If you are going to undertake criminal activities, then drown your offspring first.

You may be forming an opinion that my father and his accomplice's illegal clandestine activities meant they were out and out criminals but that is not a phrase that in any way describes my family morals.

Whilst I cannot argue that it was against the law, all they were doing was swapping one commodity for another. Apples for butter, eggs for cheese, chicken for lamb, sugar for vehicle repairs and the like.

The war was finished, and it was peacetime, so no ships were being sunk by the enemy and therefore no lives were at risk, so surely if you are trying to feed your family a variety of foods this is just community spirit and if caught very OTT to be labelled a criminal offender I would have thought.

Moving on. At some time, Dad made another of his spontaneous purchases and came home with a pure black Labrador Retriever puppy.

Very unfortunately the name we chose for this little puppy is with due justification now considered a highly racist name so from hereon in he will be referred to as Dog, hopefully, that will not offend anybody.

Dog was with us a long time and lived to be seventeen years old. Dog besides being a pet for us, was intended to have a functional use in keeping with his pedigree as a breed reared to be a gun dog.

Chris says that dad bought and trained Dog to take with him to bring back the kill when he went shooting. I can recall dad going shooting a number of times but to me Dog was far to scatty to train effectively for such a precise task. It is my view that the intention was for Dog to help gather together the geese, ducks and chickens and coax them into the runs of a night. I am not sure if this aim was ever totally successful because I have no recollection of seeing him perform this feat.

However, I do remember the hilarious training periods where he totally failed to understand his function and when released just ran completely amok scampering around among them, sending them into panic mode, with fowl of all types going off in all directions and creating total mayhem, deafening squawking and a lots of wing flapping, all of which made Dog behave even more erratic.

Dad then bought a collar and lead before trying any more training sessions. What I can remember was a successful part of the training was that you could give him the command to 'Stay', then place a treat just a few inches from his nose and he would sit staring at it for fifteen or more minutes before we'll say *'Go then'* to him and he would leap up and whoof it down before you changed your mind.

As I have said David is a great animal lover as is Chris. David would spend hours playing with Dog, rough and tumbling with him, throwing balls for him to fetch and the like. Whereas, I would spend time trying to get him to learn tricks. Despite his breed he was not the most intelligent of dogs, so it took a great deal of patience to get him to learn new ones. That said, bringing back and releasing thrown objects and sitting patiently he did master and thereby my patience was rewarded too. That said, maybe Chris was correct in that Dog did master the art of sitting patiently and when instructed scamper off to seek out the fallen prey, retrieve it and drop it at his master's feet.

Oh yes, don't let me forget the rabbits, how could I do that? Apparently, these were the result of putting ones hand up at an auction when there was only one bid, Dad's. Obviously, nobody else saw the value of this potential bargain. A lot of just two rabbits, one doe and one buck, that were soon living in a desirable coastal town residence furnished in ultimate comfort and all for free.

In the knowledge that the local housing association would always put a roof over their heads, Doe and Buck then took this once in a lifetime opportunity to do what rabbits do best and went on to produce hundreds of bunnies.

With the offspring overwhelming their residence at an alarming rate dad unexpectedly ended up making maybe five or six rabbit hutches in quick succession as each brood of babies then began to cramp their mum, dad, and siblings.

This population explosion inevitably resulted in the landlord finding it impossible to keep up with a viable building programme. Mr & Mrs Rabbit then took it upon themselves to make an increasing number of their more adult offspring homeless. These abandoned bunnies then resorted to squatting in egg laying coops, creating an unwanted conflict between them and the local fowl community.

Meanwhile other evicted and homeless bunnies took things into their own hands and started an illegal construction programme without planning permission.

They commenced building an illegal underground community of tunnels rather than wait any longer to be housed. With the inevitable result that it caused discord among the hardworking human population of our own neighbourhood.

With a doe being able to conceive at four weeks old and six litters of say five bunnies per year it did not take long before we were totally overrun with these cuddly little cuties. In the end I'm unsure if some escaped or whether Dad just let them loose in shear frustration, but it was not long before our neighbours were complaining that the unwanted immigrants were eating every green plant in sight as well as anything coloured that was edible i.e. most of the flowers and to add insult to injury they then dug great big holes in their gardens too. Dad gave the butcher *Drake the snake* permission to capture and sell any trespasser, which he willingly did and bought a new TV on the proceeds! *A Shark as well as a snake*

I must leave it there because I honestly do not have a clue as to how Mum and Dad resolved this ever-growing problem. Perhaps, Dad then imported a pack of foxes, or possibly he used a shotgun to diminish the numbers to zero or maybe that's the real reason we scooted back to London and left someone else with the problem, who knows?

The next incident was one where David got his comeuppance for his disobedience, although even to this day I think it was an extreme price to pay for what was nothing more than a minor example of defiance.

As I have intimated, Dad had spent a lot of time and effort building rabbit hutches and was finishing them off by painting them white.

He then left us somewhat suddenly, which I assume must have been for a toilet break otherwise he would have put the paint and brush in a far more secure location.

But before he left, he told us not to touch anything under any circumstances. But of course, that was red rag to bull for David and Dad had only travelled a few paces before David picked up the brush and started to complete the job for him. But being incredibly young and totally inexperienced in the trade of painting and decorating he just slapped great brush-fulls of paint everywhere other than where it was supposed to be.

Determined to finish the complete redecoration of the interior and exterior of these fine properties before Dad arrived back, he was sloshing paint around for all he was worth.

This was not household paint but limewash that was being applied to help kill off all the bugs and germs on and in the hutches in an effort to protect the rabbits from the various disease they might contract during infancy. It was not long before he managed to splash some in his eyes which made them water, which in turn caused him to wipe away the tears with his hand that was covered in paint, so that got even more in his eyes.

So now David was crying with very painful eyes and to be honest this was a bit of a godsent really because this made his eyes water even more and helped reduce the chance of permanent damage. Fortunately, Dad was soon back, and he said sharply *"You stupid boy. Why don't you ever do as you are told"* then picked him up and ran as fast as he could to the kitchen and not too gently washed his eyes out with running water from the tap.

With David, just this once in his life totally losing his *'I'm 'ard man'* persona, screamed the house down. For the next couple of days, he looked and felt a sorry sight with very red puffy eyes, but fortunately no lasting damage was done.

We were again warned that we should avoid going anywhere near the hutches for a few days to allow the paint to fully dry. With a painful lesson learnt as a reminder, David strictly adhered to these latest instructions.

When the new tenants arrived, as a reward for a rare period of good behaviour, we were then allowed to help settle these cute fluffy baby rabbits into their new abode.

Our next transgression was another where we used a considerable amount of effort transforming a simple idea into reality. It was a cleverly accomplished but absolutely stupid idea that could have had very serious consequences. I am not sure which of us it was that dreamed up this irresponsible thought, but it was obviously endorsed by both parties, because we were very enthusiastic about the idea, we soon got to work to bring the concept to reality.

This involved two kids deciding to become undersized navvies and digging a hole where a hole don't belong. This was a real effort for us for a couple of reasons. The first being that it needed to be at least a metre square and over a metre deep. The second being to scatter the excavated earth away from the area so that the digging was no longer obvious.

Once the hole was of the correct proportions, we gathered lots of sticks of sufficient length, together with straw and long grass. We then laid the sticks across the hole in crisscross fashion and covered these with the straw and grass. The result being a perfectly formed bear trap.

We were very pleased with the result because it looked exactly how we had imagined it would. All we needed now was for a bear to amble by, but we would settle for a tiger or a lion if that were all that were passing the spot at the time. We had convinced ourselves that our ingenuity, planning and hard graft, coupled with our cunning camouflage would shortly lead to us bagging a sizable prey. However, despite continuous surveillance over a longish period of time, not a single large animal of any description had fallen foul of our trap, not even a fox, which upon reflection was probably our original target. As a result, we became increasingly despondent and after a while just lost interest in the mission all together and simply moved on to the next adventure, in so doing totally forgetting the location of the trap altogether.

That is until one day while we were walking between the rows of trees with Dad, he suddenly gave out a frightening yell and fell headlong into the setup.

We just stood there stupefied, because the one captive we had not considered was Dad, and although he had just managed to demonstrate that we were indeed expert trap makers, we knew the implications at that moment was he was unlikely to fully recognise our brilliance or even be in the slightest bit pleased.

I am not sure if he was initially stunned by the fall, because it was some time before he made another sound. However, once he regained his breath, we knew we had indeed captured a very large beast that was suffering from a severely injured pride made worse by the pain of a few scratches on his person. He could have broken his leg, arm, a rib or two or any manner of other injuries, but fortunately came away more or less unscathed. Initially by his demeanour it seemed this roaring creature was about to turn his misfortune to his long-term advantage by murdering us both and burying our remains in our own pit.

Once again, because of our stupidity he had been driven to become extremely verbal and outraged. Nonetheless, his reaction was possibly more a demonstration of his increasing exasperation at his inability to get us children to use some forethought to the possible implications before blindly undertaking these mindless assignments.

We just stood looking completely remorseful while he ranted at us, not something he did very often despite our repeated transgressions. This was different though because it could have had very serious consequences indeed and therefore was totally justified.

After a while he calmed down a touch and ordered us to fill the pit in. He stood over us while we collected earth together and dropped it into the whole, while he trod it down to make it firm. Each time I looked up at him he was still shaking his head in disbelief of our thoughtlessness and regretful at having produced a pair of morons.

At this point I must return to the Jeep as promised before it gets forgotten altogether.

The passenger sat back-to-back with the self-appointed driver and custodian of transport David, a status position he always fervently defended, on the pretext that my driving was far too sedate and unexciting and to his mind not the driving style for a vehicle designed for desert warfare.

To start with I would assist with the motive power by sitting in the back pushing with my feet dangling out of the back, but this chaffed the back of my legs and made them sore, so I craftily sat cross-legged in the back and let him do all the work.

However, this ruse was short lived and soon discovered the by the self-nominated driver, now with the hurriedly added promotion to conductor, who used his new status to duly evict me from the vehicle for non-compliance with company policy.

Without my additional weight he was easily able to peddle propel the vehicle forward and managed to attain a reasonable speed.

In the meantime, I just stood there looking pitiful and abandoned and it worked, I had pulled at his heart strings and him being very considerate to my mental wellbeing, suggested if I pushed the Jeep with him in it, it would be good mental and physical therapy for me.

With him peddling for all he was worth and me pushing with like vigour, we could get up to quite a pace.

However, irrespective of the speed attained this was far too mundane for David and the former infant stunt man raised his game to become a fully-fledged kamikaze pilot and to add to the thrill did it all his feats without the aid of a pilot's helmet, goggles, seatbelt, or ejector seat!! With this level of motive power at his disposal, it was not long before we had enough oomph to attempt his stunts.

Initially this just included crashing straight into walls or other preconstructed obstacles and ramps, but his best was yet to come, and this involved sharply turning the steering wheel to full lock whilst still going at full speed, with the obvious result that the Jeep rolled onto its side and slid for a distance before grinding to a halt, with him laughing his head off.

So not surprisingly it was no longer in the beautiful pristine condition it had been just a few months before when the Christmas wrapping paper was removed.

No longer did it stand as a testament to the artistic vision, creative ingenuity, refined skills, craftmanship, time and toil our father had expended producing this fashioned toy he then lovingly entrusted to his sons.

In its original condition the jeep would have been the envy of any child, but shamefully it was now only a shadow of its former glory.

I recall dad powerfully aired his displeasure when he saw how his hard labour was being abused and made it quite clear that crashes were not part of the enjoyment package he had envisaged for his sons.

After that we were especially careful to only abuse the Jeep when he was at well out of sight and this invariably meant when he was at work.

How ungrateful can two children be! However, I don't know why I'm saying two children, I was only ever the bystander. Do not blame me, if his father could not control him, what chance did I stand.

Dad didn't have to fend off his punches whereas I did. It was necessary to comply because I just couldn't take the bruises anymore. Why should I take the rap as well milord? The answer is quite simple, if you are present when the misdemeanour takes place and you have taken even a very minor part or were present but make no attempt to prevent it, then at best you are condoning it, and at worse you are part of a conspiracy and as unfair as it may seem, in every instance you are equally guilty.

Following that convincing declaration, the only line open to me now is to accept guilt and show due remorse for how ungrateful I was as one of the two overindulged little boys that behaved abominably to the toys they received. I am therefore compelled to offer a belated but heartfelt sorry to my parents for my total lack of thought to the amount of dedication it took to ensure we were always fed, happy and provided for, which including toys and goodies that others would have given their right arm for.

I do have to conclude this piece by adding that Chris had nothing to do with this abuse of the Jeep. This was mostly because he was physically too big to get inside it. Much to his annoyance.

Whilst we are talking about Chris, I do appear to have completely left him out of my ramblings, but this is genuinely that I have very few recollections of antics we did that included him. I am trying hard not to leave the impression that he was indifferent to our antics, because I do not think he was, it is just that our idea of fun was something he had grown out of some years before. Because of the age differences his own interests did not involve his younger brothers very often.

He was as I recall just a normal boy doing what lads of his age did but being older meant playing with children his own age and not indulging in the infantile antics of his younger siblings.

While I am talking about brothers, what I have said so far makes it sound like David was just an out-of-control rascal and bully which is actually far from the truth, in reality he is and always has been a kind, caring and loving person, however a bit of a hot head.

His concept of risk starts at far higher scale than any average person and thereby he is totally fearless. OK in his early years he was quite possessive, like with the bike and the jeep. The bike was mine and the trike his, but once he mastered riding my bike the tricycle was relegated to being just a useless piece of scrap iron and the bike was then shared.

He has many traits that are very endearing and generally everybody that meets him warms to him immediately. Even, if their main comments after are, *"Your brother is such a character!"* Which he certainly is, a one off, a unique individual with no airs and graces, my hero on most occasions, but sadly an embarrassment on a number of others too. While I am in the mood for reflecting upon the family I have to say that we were incredibly lucky as children, in that during the Garage era our parents could easily afford to provide for us even though Mum never went out to work after Chris was born.

I am sure you appreciate that being a mother and housewife was a very demanding full-time job back then. There were not the aids to life we have today, no washing machine, electric iron, vacuum cleaner, microwave oven or even refrigerator, so servicing a family where everything was cleaned by hand and buying food daily so that it was always fresh meant that being a mother was far more than a full-time job.

For a long period during our life in Gt. Yarmouth we had a good lifestyle, enviable to most others of our generation, but even then, nothing comparable to that which most children consider totally normal today.

I'm not sure when it was, but it could have been during, before or after the Jeep abuse that a similar fate befell our bike.

David once again had developed a compelling desire to considerably shorten his life and this time it was by doing Evel Knievel type stunts on the bike.

Like before he again did this without any thought of adorning personal protective attire whatsoever. Obviously, this time it did mean some cuts and bruises were sustained and far too frequently for me to understand his logic in attempting the stunts in the first place.

Initially they were just little ramps raised at one end by a couple of bricks. He would push (our) his bike backwards up the ramp and I would be charged with holding the bike still while he got on it and stood on the peddles, then when instructed I had to release him, and he would fly down the ramp and through the hoop of fire - Imaginary fire that is. Well, that was the theory anyway!

Most of the times he lost control and went over the side of the plank and landed in a painful heap long before reaching the end of the ramp. But for David pain was never good reason to give up.

Of course, these failures were entirely my fault and generally due to my lack of co-ordination between the 'GO' command and the actual release, or at least that was always his perception of the reason for each failure.

His method of 'training' me was extremely simple too. He thought that administering like pain to that he had sustained would be a very educational lesson, which obviously it wasn't, and only ended up in sustained periods of communal fisticuffs.

However, once I perfected my part of the stunt, his having been perfect all along, he was able to dream up modifications like going down one ramp to give him momentum and up the next at sufficient speed to propel him off the end into space, eventually to land on the deliberately placed obstructions with sufficient force to cause their complete destruction or more often personal injury to him personally.

This 'game' got bigger and more dangerous as time went by and the ultimate stunt was then conceived.

This was a full scaffold plank balanced on a rabbit hutch to a height of about one and a half metres, then onto a pile of bricks and then another scaffold plank to the ground.

Even with me giving him my all during the assisted starts he just could not get enough oomph to power himself anywhere near the top of the ramp and off into the intended stratosphere.

Sadly, despite multiple attempts his efforts only resulted in an equal number of crashes over the side of the ramp.

Eventually with an air of shear frustration he recognised his limitations and decided he had to modify his idea of the ultimate launch.

He then decided to offer the expectant crowd a modified but nevertheless still spectacular ride 'down' the ramp as an alternative.

To add to the spectacle, we included a couple of adaptions to the original concept where now he was supposed to fly down this massive ramp as fast as his little legs would let him and then onward to demolish an even larger batch of obstacles.

His vision of receiving tumultuous applause from a highly enthusiastic crowd in recognition of a fantastic display of courage and skill was only limited by the attendance figures being restricted to just one child, me.

After much huffing and puffing and mutual verbal abuse, we did eventually manage to get the bike, rider, and crew on to the top of the hutch.

When we were ready, my perfectly timed release saw him on his way down, however he travelled probably for no more than a metre before he lost the line of travel and plunged headfirst over the side to hit the ground with an almighty bump.

The action of releasing him caused me to lose my balance too, I then wobbled about a bit but being unable to regain my self-control also toppled, managing to miss the bike, but fall very heavily on top of David instead, much to his annoyance and discomfort.

A period of joint hollering linked with attempted physical retribution caused me to switch into defence, which in my case was not to fight back but to try and stay out of reach of the intended blows while I used my major attribute, talking.

I prattled on until eventually I managed to make him see sense and realised that we had survived almost completely unscathed, a line of reasoning he very grudgingly recognised was true.

Once he accepted this and calmed down we became as usual loving brothers once again.

Although we came through this episode generally undamaged, unfortunately the same could not be said about the bike because the forks were inexplicably bent at a peculiar angle that made the bike totally unrideable.

David was bought to tears, not by the pain of his personal injuries, but by the sight of our bike. Again, I say our bike, but in reality, I was rarely allowed to ride it because it was David's pride and joy and he considered it to be HIS bike even though his own was actually a tricycle.

Enter our hero Dad, who initially spent time inspecting the twisted bike forks, then just stood there scratching his head because our explanation to how the incident caused the damage did not seem to conform to any of his scientific training he had received concerning mechanical stresses. Eventually realising that mechanical science lessons would have to wait till another time he just set about straightening the bike forks, which he did manage with little difficulty.

However further inspection showed that correcting the bent forks had weakened them and they were now suffering metal fatigue. Not one to be beaten, meant he was not going to give up and lob the whole lot in a skip. Instead set about strengthening the damage by brazing over the weakened area and then reinforcing it by adding a metal 'splint' to each arm of the fork.

The bike was then functional again, even though the results of surgery were visible for all to see. David and I were both delighted that the bike had not suffered terminal injury. In fact, it continued to be a part of our lives until we outgrew it, or it was replaced with a new one. I cannot remember which.

We then spent a major part of our outdoor activities doing our very best to wreck the rest of our toys and I'm sorry to say this included the bike.

Actually, now I think of it, destruction was not limited to external exploits. I can clearly remember David deciding to attempt a toboggan run by launching himself down the stairs whilst riding on mum's wooden tea tray. The result was obvious, a few runs led to a few bruises for David, eventual demolition of the tea tray, and chastisement from both mum and dad.

The good thing is dad did manage to replace some of the broken wood, glue together the remainder and then lacquer the whole thing, so that it ended up like new, well nearly.

Another of his ill thought out escapades one rainy day was to attach a piece of rope to the landing banister rail with the other end dangling above the stairs, then attempting to climb up to the landing like a mountain climber. Again, a few bruises resulted. Mum fortunately arrived to see what the commotion was and immediately intervened to ensure this did not result in any broken bones. Being squeamish, I had long since deserted him and was probably doing drawing in my room as the alternative to watching him kill himself.

Apologies for the totally random order of these tales but I have once again gone off in a totally new direction. It was coming up to Mum's birthday, or at least I think it was some such like occasion.

David and I decided it would be a great idea if we could make her a beautiful Tea trolley as a present.

We initially rummaged through Dad's stock of wood materials and using our undeniable knowledge of timber, selected wood of the highest premium quality to incorporate within this product of sheer excellence.

We then needed tools and having not yet perfected the art of lock picking, used a table knife to unscrew the hinges to Dad's new workshop.

Believing the substantial hasp and staple secured by a combination padlock would make the recently constructed building impenetrable dad had not bothered to lock the tools. Once we were into dad's fortress, we were able to gather a saw, hammer, hand brace, drill bits, screws, nuts and bolts and a vision in our minds of how to turn this superb idea into reality. I think all must have been going well, until we got to the part in the design where we needed to drill a hole in a piece of metal. An appropriately size twist drill was selected, which I know was blooming big, so something like twelve mm diameter.

Remember electric hand drills had not been invented yet, actually in reality no electric hand tools of any type were available. Mr. Black and Mr. Decker were yet to arrive on the scene.

We fitted the bit into the manual drill brace, and I was assigned the task or turning the brace while David sitting cross legged on the ground holding the piece of metal on top of a piece of wood.

However, drilling a piece of metal with a hand brace was always going to be difficult even to an adult. An adult may have had the wherewithal to select a smaller drill and make a pilot hole first.

I started off turning gently at first but after a minute or two had made no impression whatsoever, not so much as a mark even.

I was then encouraged by my co-conspirator to press harder, which I did and then even harder until I was pressing with all my might and then suddenly the drill slipped - Now take a deep breath, please.

I had managed to hit David's leg about a fifteen cm above his knee on the inside of his leg and this was a serious size wound and I mean serious.

I just stood there mortified and looking at his sizable wound, whereas David didn't scream but just sat there mesmerized for a moment or two before suddenly leaping up and going into a total rage, grabbed a hammer and with the intent of killing the idiot brother, chased me for quite a distance before the pain kicked in and he collapsed with blood spurting out of his leg.

Even today I can vividly remember this horrific accident and describing it now still makes me feel a little queasy.

However, as traumatic as this episode was at the time, I cannot now say how it concluded. He certainly needed stitches, but this was another occasion like all others before or after where we never went to hospital to repair our wounds.

There was hell to pay afterwards, because whilst Dad was at work we had managed once again to get up to total mischief without our warder at least peeping in from time to time to see what we were up to. This was another instance where dad let rip with his tongue before thinking it through. I am sure he would prefer to have come home to a cooked meal and clean bedsheets than a tale of how mum had approved, supervised, and recorded all our daily activities so that he could be judge to her performance in this task when he arrived home.

I still say it was all dad's fault anyway, because given that we were totally untrustworthy, he should have confined us to an escape proof cell until he arrived home to let us out and then supervise us. However, I am not so sure that was an answer anyway, because some of our wayward doings occurred of a weekend while he was at home and our supervisor in any case.

As for Mum not supervising us sufficiently, you should know that she had three sons that were without doubt the dirtiest little urchins ever and a husband that was not a lot better, he worked as a motor mechanic and had a subconscious desire to wipe his greasy hand down his overalls. There were always clothes to be cleaned and in this family a bit more than just a few. Add in bedclothes, towels, tea cloths and the like, that together needed to go through the washing machine.

The washing machine operator was Mum, and only mum. This machine was armed with a skiffle board, a bar of carbolic soap, a stiff brush and a great deal of elbow grease powered by her too.

After which the clean washing needed to be put through the mangle to remove some of the water by mum, hung to dry by mum, ironed with a flat iron by mum, folded and put away also by mum.

I should add that this routine was carried out in a butler sink and the water heated in a large double handled vessel that was carted back and forth between the butler sink and the kitchen range. The water got changed when it either got cold or became too dirty to be of further use.

The mangle was also hand driven by this sole washer woman using the crank handle and to add to her woes, the flat iron was heated by placing it on the range every time it cooled below the ideal temperature for removing creases, which was every minute or so.

On top of all that she had to pick up all the mats, take them outside beat them with a beater, wet mop, then dry and polish all the floors, pop out and buy food, cook it, serve it, and then wash up and put away all the utensils, crockery, and cutlery.

Surely given her efficiency at carrying out the described domestic tasks, it is unreasonable for anyone to expect her to be equally competent at managing her offspring.

Being mindful of the whereabouts of each of her sons throughout every second of the day and with that provide adequate supervision to ensure their activities remained within the standards set, was according to Dad just a normal part of her daily domestic duties. Or at least that was the totally unreasonable view expressed by him occasionally, before being shot down in flames and soon regretting having uttered his ill-chosen words.

I may have left the impression here that dad was a control freak that totally dominated our mum. Far from it, on the occasions he was silly enough to air a singular view on any subject, he would very soon regret it and remember who was boss in our house and on which side his bread was buttered.

The range was a very efficient multi-function heating device that stood in the fireplace in our kitchen. The area surrounding the fireplace was clad all over with light green painted tongue and groove wooden boards which was in vogue during that period.

The range besides heating the water, was also the sole means of cooking, as well as warming the kitchen. It had two ovens for cooking with the lids doubling up as hobs. It was a truly universal appliance with one small drawback, which was that on washing days the water reservoir was insufficient to supply enough for the mass of washing that needed to be cleaned.

When adverse weather prevented fresh air clothes drying the best alternative place was of course anywhere above the range. There was a clothes dryer suspended from the ceiling above the range which comprised of four wooden poles laid horizontally and held apart by a spacer piece at either end. The wet clothes were placed over the rods and a rope and pully system allowed the whole thing to be raised and lowered as required.

Central Heating was not yet common in most people's houses so each other room had a fireplace where coal was used as the fuel to heat each individual room. The range also being coal fired was obviously not an on/off energy source like gas or electricity, it could be controlled within limits, by restricting or releasing the flow of air through it and thereby the intensity of the combustion.

However, it did take time for the range to respond to these control changes, and even when the heat output had been regulated, the body still got very hot, which meant we needed a sturdy fixed fire guard enclosing all sides of it to prevent any of us coming into contact with it and burning ourselves.

In this instance Mum and Dad had provided a well thought out strong system to reduce the risk of injury to their family and visitors. These were securely fitted to unsure the health and safety requirements were more than adequate if adhered to. However, not everyone seemed to appreciate the robust benefits the installed precautions provided.

Enter David, a Health and Safety Officers nightmare, a rogue dis-believer in all things safe, who considered that these precautions had been provided more as a welcome aid to help in his quest of following dangerous pursuits than as a means of defence from them. On this occasion he used a chair to stand on and this gave him the height to step onto the top edge of the fire guard and then standing on tip toe, almost provided sufficient lift for him to reach whatever it was on the mantlepiece that attracted his attention in the first place. However, this particular day, nearly was not quite enough, so just another little stretch up was needed, and that try was one try too far.

With arms flapping around in all directions like a tight-rope walker he attempted to regain his balance, but the forces of nature intervene, and he tumbled, not onto the quarry tile floor to fracture his skull, but directly onto the top of the range.

He landed with his right thigh directly onto the red-hot hob, and in a split second, he leapt up screaming in pain. However, even though he was barely on the range a second, he did sustain a very nasty burn over a large area of his right thigh. He was screaming in agony and mum was there in a flash, lifted him to the sink and directed the cold tap to the spot to remove some of the heat. The injury was then dressed with some of mums magic cream and bandaged up.

I have still got a graphic mind's eye picture of him having a great big gauze pad held in place by sticking plaster and him walking like a zombie in a stiff legged strut for quite a while after. He still has the scar to this day.

He was not taken to hospital on this occasion either and again you may wonder why?

As you know the NHS was only formed in 1948. Prior to which hospitals were vastly different to those we know today. We arrived to live in Gt. Yarmouth before the NHS had commenced and it was still in its infancy when we left there.

Prior to then hospitals were funded by charitable donations, patients' contributions, and partially by some local councils.

This meant that there were vast differences between the availability, quality, and expertise hospitals provided at that time.

There certainly was not an accident and emergency department in many. This produced a longstanding mindset that one should try to deal with the matter themselves or pay for a doctor to call and deal with an emergency if one was available. The longstanding view that doctors and hospitals should be avoided unless it was a life-threatening situation remained the view of most people for a considerable number of years after the formation of the NHS free medical care policy.

That said, I did twice have operations in Great Ormond Street hospital for Children and once in Norwich General, but I was very young at the time. These were totally necessary medical problems, but I have no idea how they were administrated or even who paid for the facilities.

Whilst writing this story I have spent considerable amounts of time trying to link one event to the next in an attempt to make it flow, but I have to admit, without any great success. Please excuse this next jump to a totally new planet.

Even though the house had three rooms downstairs, one of these was Dad's 'work' room.

The other two although nicely furnished rooms were rarely used for recreation. Strangely when adverse weather forced us to retreat to a more pleasing indoor environment we would choose the kitchen. If we were forced indoors, it was there that we spent nearly all our leisure time.

In the middle of the kitchen there was a big white enamel topped table, the primary function of this being to act as the food prep area, but it also served many other purposes too. One of which was as our 'games' area, a favourite one being to draw roads in pencil directly onto the white enamel tabletop so that we had a proper layout for our toy cars. Mum was not overly keen on us drawing on the tabletop because she was the one that ultimately had to clean it off afterwards, so she would get annoyed if we introduced too much detail to outline our perception of a town.

I can say that designing roadways and moving cars about was one time when Chris would join in quite eagerly with David and me. Which has triggered me to recollect that he also loved to draw war scenes not on the table but on paper, and he would spend hours doing action drawings of British spitfires chasing German Messerschmitt's or Focke-Wulf's - Don't ask me to pronounce this please.

With the Huns in flames and diving into the sea the Brits were always the winners to his mind.

As you can see demonstrated here, we were not always the totally out of control pocket-sized hooligans the rest of this set of my tales have portrayed. That said, you may not be convinced and want to revert to your previous assessment. If not before, I'm pretty sure you will when you read and consider the antics we perpetually got up to as children, through adolescence and even as adults.

While still on the kitchen theme I need to tell you about the next event that occurred there. It is again an awfully close call episode. One that could easily have had devastating consequences and changed the make-up of our family from that moment and forever after.

This one does not originate from anything the usual culprits did, but most surprisingly from their father, yep, the person who was always very quick to point out their frequent flaws when his otherwise beloved sons failed to conform to the minimum standards asked of them.

Early one morning 'Dog' was in his usual bed below the kitchen table, but suddenly started barking furiously. David without waking anyone else, went to investigate and immediately raced back upstairs shouting *"Mum, Mum, quick get up there is lots of smoke in the kitchen."*

It seems that when David had gone downstairs to investigate why the dog was agitated, he opened the door to find the kitchen was on fire. His first thought was to rescue his beloved pet 'Dog', so fearing the worst he called his name and much to his relief 'Dog' scampered out, so Dave then quickly closed the door and raced back upstairs to raise the alarm.

Mum was obviously out of bed in a split second and told him to get me and Chris up too.

Apparently, Dad had lit a cigarette as his last act before leaving for work and tossed the match into the open top on the range, or at least he thought he had, but missed and instead it had landed on top of a tea cloth that had fallen from the clothes dryer and was then laying in the hearth, where it started to burn.

This mini fire then caught the remaining clothes on the dryer so that it escalated to the wooden cladding of the fireplace, and once the paint ignited, the fire quickly accelerated such that a full inferno was under way.

We were ordered to stay in the porch and not move, while Mum dealt with the situation. Mum said that she cautiously opened the door and was immediately struck in terror at the extent of the fire and knew that unless she acted quickly the result would be catastrophic.

With visions of losing the whole house and everything in it, she took a deep breath, rushed into the kitchen, grabbed a towel to wrap round her face, turned on the taps and with a washing bowl started pitching water in the general direction of the fire.

Having first had the forethought to put the plug in the sink meant that there was soon enough water for her to scoop and throw almost full bowls at the inferno. She said that due to the smoke she was coughing and spluttering almost immediately and was soon faced with the dilemma, whether to open the back door to let the smoke out, although she knew this would increase the fire or to brave it out and hope to be able to breath until she had extinguished the fire. She opened the door.

Meanwhile we were terrified that Mum might be in danger, so we went back to see if she was OK. Upon opening the door, she bellowed at us to go back and close the door again, which we reluctantly did.

It seemed like an eternity before she came out, staggered to the stairs, sat down heavily, and coughed and coughed. We all ran too her and cuddled up to her in sheer relief. Mum, then just burst into uncontrollable tears. This was probably a combination of her choking, the trauma of fighting the fire and her vision of what might have been had her attempts been in vain. Such was her distress that we collectively joined her sorrow. Probably two thirds to the left of the wood panelling was charred, the remainder of the paint was all bubbled up, the whole of the ceiling was black as was the remaining walls.

One thing I never quite understood was why Mum didn't get Chris to run to the fire station which was only a hundred metres away and get them to take over from her. Possible in her traumatic state she was not thinking clearly. Which is quite understandable.

Mum did say after the trauma had subsided, she had thought of taking us all with her to a phone box to phone Dad at the garage and get him to come home but realised there was little he could do at that moment anyway, so there was no point.

I imagine upon seeing the level of devastation a careless toss of a match had caused he would have reflected long and hard upon how it might have turned out and although thankful would have been duly sorry for mum's trauma while fighting the fire.

Remaining on the subject thoughtlessness, one would have thought that given the number of times David and I had managed to entertain ourselves by utilising objects not intended as playthings, anything that was not suitable for that purpose would have been better stored safely in a David proof, strong metal container or impenetrable building.

In view of this the next couple of events are ones where the objects involved would have been better placed under lock and key.

The first was a large container of something like 10 litres capacity, with a conical top, obviously shaped to help with poring its contents. It was capped with an exceptionally large cork.

I think Dad must have placed it by his tool shed the previous day, because its unexpected arrival was what kindled our curiosity in the first place.

I think I must take the unusual step of admitting to complicity during this next misdemeanour of ours because I was certainly involved during the initial stages.

Much to our surprise we were able to remove the cork with ease. After which our first thought was to tip it so we could pour out a small quantity for analysis.

However, the container was too heavy for us to lift or even tilt, so we tried to peer down through the neck and see if we could see what it was, but it was so dark inside all we could see was black.

I then had the brilliant idea of using a piece of rope that was lying on the ground close bye and dropping this down through the neck and when withdrawing it to see if we could determine what it was.

My first attempt came back with nothing, so David snatched it from me and had a go, but in his case, he didn't stop until all of the rope was inside the drum except the bit he was holding on to.

As he pulled it out, we could see that it was some sort of black substance. I then pointed out that he was getting it all over his hands and down his trousers, but typical David, he was not perturbed and just carried on. I unwisely decided to remonstrate with him, which just made matters worse because he then started to twirl the rope round his head sending this substance in all directions.

I then decide to step in a try to grab it from him, but he resisted, and this was followed by a period of us grappling with each other, until I lost the battle and retreated with him chasing me all the way to the kitchen.

A sudden *"What the hell do you think you are doing?"* from Mum stopped the chase. *"What is it and where did you get it?"* our explanation was met with *"Oh, my god that's Dad's tar that he needs to seal the tool shed roof."* So, there were these two little boys covered in black tar from head to toe and desperately in need of a good wash. But, if you have ever tried to clean tar from anything you will know that it is an almost impossible task. Petrol seemed to be the only thing that could get the tar out of our hair and off our bodies. This had to wait until Dad got home and syphoned some from the car. We were told to take our clothes off and then put them back on inside out to avoid soiling anything. We were banned from the house and forced to sit in the garden and await his arrival. We were then stood it the bath and scrubbed down with the petrol and a pumice stone then bathed in hot water.

Being rubbed down with the stone made our skin quite sore so we then had to endure having lard rubbed on our bare bodies. Moisturisers or body creams of any type were not available until many years later, so this less than effective alternative was the best solution on offer at the time. Cleaning our clothes proved to be an impossible task thought, so they were simply discarded and burnt.

What I am about to relay to you now has nothing to do with any of the previous incidents, but this and several others yet to come are related by one common factor, bullying. This is a subject very much in the public eye at present, which leave me wondering if bullying remains a yet to be eradicated problem at the time you are reading this.

As you are probably aware all bullies completely avoid strong and active individuals because that person may fight back or offer a reciprocal verbal response they cannot handle. They instead pick upon the physically weak or mentally fragile members of our society. As I mentioned earlier, I was an asthma sufferer and as a result unintentionally gave off a weak and frail persona, not helped by me being incredibly shy and fearful of all confrontation anyway. The first of many future described incidents starts with a totally innocuous minor accident.

We were just leaving school for the day and as I was running out of the gate, I looked back to see where David was, but he was not behind me as I expected. Such was my hurry and inattention I accidently bumped into a lad walking by on the pavement outside. This was truly just a minor little bump and could not have caused him any injury at all, but despite my continued and desperate apologies, he reacted in a totally over the top manner. He grabbed me by the coat collar, swung me round and slammed me against the brick gate post and started shouting expletives at me just inches from my face.

To make things worse for me, his friend realising I was otherwise occupied and unlikely to resist, took the cowardly opportunity to use me as a punchbag even though the original bully had the job well under control and needed no further help.

This commotion obstructed the gateway and prevented my school friends from passing.

They were yelling for the lads to stop when David forced through and pushed the lad punching me so hard that he fell over backwards.

Before the other bully could react, David punched him in the side of the face and as he turned David gave him another punch straight on the mouth.

The one on the ground tried to drag my brother down by grabbing his leg, but he managed to shake him off and in so doing caught him in the mouth with his heel. They both did no more than get up and scamper away. Possibly they had learnt to think carefully before picking on an apparent sucker target in future in case he too had a minder behind him as back-up.

It was only a few days later that we were coming out of school and the same two were walking along on the other side of the road.

David was all for going after them again and I was holding him back, pleading he did not have the element of surprise this time. Fortunately, the traffic prevented us from crossing the road, but our 'discussion' attracted the bully's attention and upon realising it was us, they shot off like jack rabbits, never to be seen again that I can recall. It is worthy of mention that these two lads were older and bigger than me, otherwise I am very sure they would not have picked on me.

David was for a few years the same height and build as me, but there again not really any bigger than most others his age.

You can possibly understand why I and his school mates to boot, considered his action of wading in to defend the underdog, nothing short of Superman status.

Was then, still is, my hero brother despite his many shortcomings. As you will find out later, if only he had been available on every occasion like this that I needed him then I might have been spared a life-threatening episode.

I am now about to describe a new episode that collectively relabels all previous capers as very minor indiscretions. I have already spoken about the big garden, field, orchard, or other description I may have used to define the large piece of land beyond the rose garden at the back of our Gt. Yarmouth house. Let us call this the field, so that you are aware of the area I am referring to.

This expanse of land was, apart from the housing for fowl and rabbits, generally covered in wild grass and weeds, which you may remember from an earlier incident, tended to grow to a considerable height.

Even given that we trampled it and the fowl pecked and fed from it, there still remained a vast amount that stayed intact and could be cut, dried and used for bedding the fowl and rabbits.

Mechanical mowing was not an option, given the era we are discussing here, and in any case a mower would have cut the grass into very small pieces that would have been totally unsuitable as bedding.

Dad used to use a combination of sickle and scythe to cut the grass and weeds and for obvious reasons we needed to be well in front of him when he was cutting.

The scythe was used to swiftly cut the open areas and the sickle to cut closer around the trees and plants.

I recollect Dad letting Chris have a go with both the sickle and the scythe, but he would not let us try because both are very dangerous implements that need to be used with care, not something David and I were famed for.

I think Dad may have borrowed the sickle and scythe, or had it stored in a bank vault somewhere, otherwise I feel sure the Mayer hooligans would have dynamited the door to gain access to these two very sharp and highly dangerous tools.

Anyway, after mowing, the cuttings needed to be left to dry for a day of so, but after that I know that we all used to get involved with gathering it up into heaps, putting it in to the wheelbarrow and then piling it up in the barn. I am reasonably sure this was how it was on the occasion I am about to expand upon. By the time we had finished, the cuttings were piled to the roof and across the full width of the barn, so this was an enormous quantity of hay.

A day or so later David and I were playing quite normally in the field when we decided to gather up the miniscule amounts of the cuttings that remained on the ground and put them into little piles, and it was not long before we had reasonable sized heaps of dried hay, dotted about the field.

Mum then called us for lunch and when we returned David suddenly produced a box of matches, which either Mum or Dad had left lying about.

So, first match struck, first heap lit, and within a few seconds that pile of hay was consumed, and the flames quickly died out. However, we were not totally put off by the short duration of our small pyre displays and instead gathered several small piles of hay together and used them to make into mini bonfires. Although more satisfying, they still lasted no more than a few seconds.

The previous days efforts of cutting and storing the hay was a very efficient operation, because of which it was not long before we were finding it difficult to amass enough from what remained on the ground to make a decent display.

I then thought it might just be easier if we grabbed handfuls from the barn to construct our bonfires, which David agreed would be easier and we then busied ourselves for a while doing just that.

After a few largish bonfires we had made a very noticeable dent in the pile of stock hay in the barn.

It was then that I realised that this had to stop because without doubt we were already going to be in serious trouble when dad saw the diminished pile and worked out the reason. A heated debate then ensued because he wanted to carry on, so I then tried to snatch the matches from him. After a bit of grappling, pushing, and shoving he broke free and to my horror took a match from the box and waved it in front of me in provocation.

Terrified as to what he might do I went after him again, wrestled with him and tried to grab the match, but even though I had him in a bear hug, he managed to strike the match. It is at this point that his version differs from mine. Mine being he deliberately threw the match onto the heap in the barn and his is that I knocked it out of his hand during the struggle. You decide! Whichever debate was correct the result was the same, from where it started the fire spread rapidly, and like a pebble thrown into a pond the flames rippled across the pile and spread in ever increasing circles until within literally just a few seconds of this single match hitting the base, the whole face layer of the hay was ablaze in all directions.

This heap was probably three metres high and maybe eight metres wide and it was all burning fiercely.

Being the intelligent one, (Don't laugh) I realised that we needed water and we need it now, so I sprinted for all I was worth to the only place I could think of that had any, the kitchen.

I had a sigh of relief when I saw two milk bottles standing on the windowsill and as a bonus they were already full of water, so a grabbed them and was sprinting back when Dave caught up with me and declared that further resistance was futile.

The Great fire of Yarmouth was now consuming everything in its path, would destruct the complete town, and maybe the whole country.

With a rare flash of wisdom, he advised that such was our plight, we should with great haste, now head for the port, stowaway on a ship and sail off to a distant land that did not have an extradition treaty with the UK. After a short debate we elected to hide in the coal cupboard and await our fate. In the meantime, Mum could see the smoke and had gone to investigate only to find the fire brigade were already there attempting to reduce the damage to the minimum possible. I think the shock of how quickly the situation had escalated caused us to just sit there in the total darkness afraid to even whisper in case we blew our feeble cover. Because there was no barking evidence of a dog tracker team in hot pursuit, the search for the felons did not appear to be underway just yet.

Add together the combination; that capture was certain, the agonizingly long silence, my vision to the level of carnage created, which combined to leave me distraught. It must be how it feels to be in the USA sitting in your cell on death row.

Stupidly, I had gone along with the total idiocy of this caper and now sat trembling in terror trying to envisage the severity of the impending punishment yet to come.

I had heard that arson was a capital offence punishable by hanging by the neck till dead. I could only hope this judgement did not apply to minors.

Throughout we had been listening intently for some sign of movement, when suddenly our hearts jumped because we knew we had detected a faint faraway murmur, being unable to see David I grabbed his arm and he whispered *"shush"* as we continued to sit and hold our breaths, but it was not long before the murmurs came distinctive voices and shortly were directly outside our lair.

We knew at that moment we had been rumbled. Realising it was now far too late to make a run for it we decided to freeze and hope it would all be just a dream that would go away when we woke up.

Then Mums voice, *"You'll find them in there"*, and as the thirty pieces of silver changed hands the door swung open, and a man's voice bellowed, *"OUT!"*

A forceful command like that is impossible to disobey. Pushing one another to ensure the other was first in the firing line we reluctantly crept from the darkness, squinting from the contrasting sunlight, sobbing streams of tears and with heads bowed in shame. There the two arsonists stood to await their fate, and each muttered a hardly audible *"Sorry"* in a futile plea for leniency.

Our captor being totally unmoved by our belated regret, bawled another stern command *"YOU TWO LOOK AT ME NOW"* I slowly lifted my eyes to see a pair of very large heavy black boots leading into yellow waterproof leggings and upward to a navy-blue jacket, belt with a big hatchet and finally an absolute giant of a fireman topped off by a black helmet with three yellow stripes. The hatchet bothered me because it did look large and sharp, and made me wondered if it might have a use as an alternative to the noose.

If I had been frightened before I now felt totally petrified and even this does not truly describe my feelings at that moment. *"I am going to take you to see the result of your stupidity and let you reflect upon what might have happened had the fire station not been just across the road!"* Roared the Chief Fire Officer.

I looked across at Mum still hoping for a little bit of moral support but, still chinking her silver coins, her return look was one of great disappointment and I knew that this was the final straw and meant we were likely to be incarcerated, banished from, and totally abandoned by the family. From here on in we would be tantamount to orphans and entirely on our own for senseless reasons of our own creation.

I was quaking in fear and found my spindly legs wobbling like jellies as we were then frog marched to the crime scene.

We were totally taken aback when confronted with this complete devastation of our making. The left side of the barn where the hay had been stored was now just a pile of cinders and charred shards of wood.

The small amount of the hay that remained had

been raked out of the barn by the firemen and was now laid strewn around, wet, charred and totally useless as animal bedding or any other function.

The fire had also engulfed the damson trees closest to the barn. The adjacent one now having no leaves at all, was left in a deeply sorry state, in fact it had lost all its small branches too and stood there as a scorched barren wooden skeleton and seemed unlikely to survive. Of the other two trees that had become embroiled in the inferno one had very few leaves remaining, and numerous charred branches and the other had suffered too, but to a far lesser extent.

These three trees that previous stood tall and proud as the kings of the orchard were now looking very forlorn and unloved. The right side of barn structure although showing signs of suffering from the fire appeared in in the main to be generally intact and secure. What remained of our previous play area had been reduced to something akin to the scene from a war zone with the strike of one match. One remorseful little boy stood side by side with his equally ashamed but traumatised older brother as they stood totally transfixed by the vision before them.

We were witnessing the power that can result when a single flame expands to be become an inferno destroying everything in its path. Some seventy years later this image is still permanently etched into our brains, such that we can both recall the sight as if it happened yesterday.

Us having never seen the effects of fire, even on film, found the visual shock totally devastating and very effective at blocking out every stern word the Fire

Chief said. As such that they just faded away to become distant background mutterings and failed to make any lasting register in our brains. This mental block means that today neither of us can recall a word he said although we do have a memory of it not being very complementary. Surprisingly we cannot now convey any thought as to what Dad said or indeed what punishment we received for our criminal activity, even though criminal it certainly was.

As I say we are somewhat unsure as to what happened next, but what we do know it that it did mean a section of new fence and a barn refurbishment that resulted in a reduction of this building to not much bigger than a large garden shed. The trees did actually grow again and a year or so later seemed none the worse for having undergone an extremely severe form of pruning. All the bonfires we had seen before, like those on firework night, had taken a while to get going but once up and going did consume a great deal of material in a very short space of time. What totally astounded us was the rapid rate at which the fire developed in this case. That remains the permanent vision I have of this regrettable scene. It continues to haunt me to this day. Those first few seconds before I ran to get water, just standing there stupefied and absolutely awestruck at the speed that the fire was taking hold, and then reacting as it became obvious that without rapid intervention everything was going to be consumed. Too late, it was!

This is a good point to say that for each of our previous thoughtlessly executed exploits, Dad did not usually react like a mad bull, but was generally calm and collected even though inside he was probably finding it difficult to contain his fury.

His philosophy most often included priest like sermons designed to educate us into comprehending why our actions were totally unacceptable.

These talks continued unabated until he got a strong affirmative response to the *"Do you understand,"* question, at which point he would be left with a glimmer of hope that we might retain the salient point of his lecture and that things would change.

There were other occasions, and these were usually when injury or wanton destruction could have or did result, when the tone and volume of his dialogue did certainly indicate that we had overstepped the mark by a very considerable margin, the inferno being one of those. Nonetheless, regardless of the stupidity of any incident that we had considered to be no more serious than a prank, at no time did he ever lay hands upon us or even seem likely to. Although to be perfectly honest he could have pleaded and would have received a full pardon for the extreme provocation he had endured had he chosen to vent his displeasure in this manner.

I add that when punishment needed administering Dad would be left to deal with the most serious cases, while mum would administer a single slap across the back of the legs for the more minor misdemeanours, but there again no more than that.

It is now you can see that it was the tutoring methods used by our father to guide us through life that had a direct bearing in making us all the fine upstanding citizens we are today.

I take it you are not convinced with that statement, and I cannot blame you, because to my mind we always fell short of that expectation by a very wide margin. It was not for the want of trying on his part but more our failure to comprehend what was being asked of us.

There are many instances where my character, David's, and Chris's too, differed considerably and this is how it is even to this day.

Whereas David always seemed to have the attitude that even though he knew his capers could be construed as pure mischief, that was never good reason to abandon them, but he was always prepared, if caught, to take any punishment administered. I therefore have to say in admiration that he always took his chastisement like a man, whereas I always became a blubbering wreck pleading total sorrow and begging forgiveness.

While we are on the subject, Chris never ever did anything wrong and would continue to adamantly plead such in feigned total innocence, for each and every offence, even when caught with his hand in the safe and his fingerprints on the smoking gun in his hand.

Several dramatic changes then befell us at this point in our lives. The first of which is that Dad was forced to give up the garage business. I say forced because I am sure he would not have done so willingly, hence it must have been under great duress.

However, I and for that matter neither Chris nor David knows of the full reasons that R&M Motors Ltd. ceased to carry on trading. We do have a small notion that Bob, Mr Rilling the R in R&M, became increasingly unhappy with Gt. Yarmouth and longed to return to London, which finally came to a head when he left for London suddenly, never to return.

The garage was a registered limited company that had three equal shareholders, Bob, Dad and the third was Mr Frederick Mahringer. Our limited knowledge on the events that took place, leads us to surmise several thoughts. We know that Fred was the son of a wealthy businessman that owned a number of bakeries in North London and it is highly likely that he supplied the original capital to buy the previously defunct garage business. We do know that Fred, Bob and dad were really good long-term buddies although Fred was never involved with the day to day running of the company. Again assuming, if Dad had been expressing his displeasure at the imbalance of effort between him and Bob, then maybe things came to a head and Bob decided to shoot down to London and talk it over with Fred using his biased point of view. The result being that Fred's dad then withdrew his capital, leaving Dad to find a new backer. But that's a big maybe.

Assuming that R & M Motors had been trading profitably its market value would have increased, making it more difficult for Dad to have gone it alone and buy out the other two directors, I think their actions were therefore a fait accompli leaving Dad with no choice but to pull out.

After the garage business ceased, one thing I can remember was him bringing home a lot of the then redundant office stationery, which I delighted in playing with for some time after.

Writing out fake invoices and rubber stamping the receipts and generally 'running' the garage again.

I note that the 'R' in the R & M Motors rubber stamp had been removed and on all of the stationery it was obliterated by a black marker which by no stretch of the imagination adds to the suspicion that all was not well between him and Bob.

In fact, I do not believe they ever spoke again. Dad was the sort of person that went to the ends of the earth to help his friends but became very vindictive if crossed by them as I will explain in latter parts of this story.

Other than receiving redundant garage effects to play with I cannot say that the demise of the garage materially affected us children at that time.

Nevertheless, it did have a great affect upon the day to day lives of our parents and as I will now try to express in simple terms it was a time that changed the course of our family history forever.

If you consider this carefully you will have to see that even the most commonplace happenings in all of our lives do actually have a momentous affect in shaping our future existence.

Our location at any moment in time, who we meet and when we met, what we said, and their reply, although seemingly extremely minor daily occurrences conspire to formulate our whole lives in minute detail.

My thoughts are that whilst we have control when selecting our location at any specific moment in time, by coinciding this with a like choice by another shapes our complete future path.

Had my grandparents not immigrated to Great Britain, my mother not worked at my grandfather's factory, my father not given up the garage, our family not moved to Enfield, our part of the family not moved to Worthing; then all our lives would have had a far differing life landscape to that of today.

These are just a few of the actions my forebears, my immediate family and I took that have wholly shaped not just my life but many others too!

Had we not been there, had we not spoken to a particular person at a specific moment in time and that initial conversation had not led to a courtship and eventual integration into to our family, etc. etc. then maybe we would be living a different existence or not have been born at all.

Anyway, enough of the heavy stuff. This period in our lives is another where I am very much in the dark and having to make some suppositions in order to give clarity to the history of the events that follow and the path our lives took from there until now.

It seems that Dad's share of the money from the proceeds of the garage was sufficient for there not to be any great financial concerns, so initially life went on much as normal.

Dad, then joined a company called, Baldrey and Hatch, who I believe manufactured and serviced weighing scales. Not the electronic display type you see today but the balance type where one placed a series of ever decreasing weights in one bowl until balance agreed with the item to be weighed in the other bowl.

Although Dad was a mechanical engineer, I am not sure what his initial role was in this company, however he did buy into this business at some point. I think he felt that Baldry and Hatch were two good guys he could trust, and this friendship led him to believe that he should put all his money into the company on what later proved to be a costly impulsive whim.

I did discuss this with Mum at some time and she did say that they had a heated debate about this at the time, but Dad was adamant that this was his way to move us upward again. Whereas, when he joined into the garage venture it had all been signed and sealed with legal documents fully detailing the agreement and finances, but it does not appear that this was the case with the weighing scale venture.

Things are a bit grey here as to when or how this venture got started, but one thing is for certain, getting involved was certainly a catastrophic decision because it was not long before the company went bust.

I know there was a lot of legal debate afterwards and a court case, but I do not have enough knowledge to speculate about the outcome other than Mum saying the subsequent legal costs wiped out what little money they had left.

As I commented to in an earlier paragraph, Nanny Mayer & Auntie Julie came to visit us a couple of times while we were in Gt. Yarmouth and I believe we also went to see them in London once or twice.

Well, I know we did at least once, and it is on that trip back to see them that I recall another David incident. Although I am not at all certain, it is possible that this particular visit was around the time that Dad split up with the garage. During this visit we went by car to see the people at Shunic Limited, the company Dad worked for before he left them to start up the garage. It is possible that he was there to see if he could get a job working in their organisation once again, but that is just pure speculation on my part. The factory was close to the Dartmouth Park area of north London not very far from Highgate where Dick Whittington sat on the stone and then decided to return to London.

Anyway, back to the story. The factory was sited in Tremlett Grove which was a narrow, cobblestone clad road on a steep hill with a mishmash of old, almost primeval, industrial buildings on either side of what was not more than a lane, with Shunic's being almost at the top of this.

Dad had driven up, with the car creaking and squeaking in protest, and us too subjected to a similar bone-shaking journey to the top. Dad then turned the car round and parked it facing down the hill. While we waited in the car he went inside to have a chat with these ex-colleagues once again.

I think Mum initially stayed in the car with us boys but was then asked to go in and say hello, so she went inside, and as she left, she said *"Watch him, and do not touch anything."* – There is a red rag statement, if ever I saw one? Almost immediately David scrambled over into the front with Chris trying to pull him back by hanging on to one leg, but David just kicked out until Chris let him go. Initially all he did was stand on the driver's seat, hold on to the driving wheel and pretended to drive, which Chris considered to be a safe option, so left him alone.

Shortly after one of the men that knew Chris from the earlier London days when dad had taken him there, came over to talk to him and they were chatting when suddenly the car started to roll forward.

David with his usual lack of foresight had decided that pretending to steer was quite unexciting and having spent at least five minutes on his very own intensive driver training course, decided now was the time to put it all into practice by adding a bit of realism to his driving skills, so he released the handbrake and was ready to roll.

The guy's first thought was to try to hold the car back, but he did not have enough strength, so he then leapt onto the running board and tried to open the passenger door while shouting at Chris to pull the hand brake up again. However, try as he might Chris was impeded by having to stretch through the small gap between the seats and in that position he just did not have the strength to wrench the brake hard on.

We were now moving at a fair speed down the hill, while all the time the car was shuddering and bumping over the cobbles and this threatened to throw our rescuer off at any moment, until eventually he did manage to get the door open, and with a determined effort lean in, roughly thrust David onto the passenger seat and with a wrench of the steering wheel pointed the car into what he considered to be the softest crash barrier available, a pile of wooden pallets that were very fortuitously stacked against the wall.

This extremely dramatic situation of a ton of out-of-control runaway motor car jerking and jolting along a path toward probable untold destruction and personal injury was now being checked by a succession of pallets each of which was being unceremoniously crunched into small splinters of matchwood before our very eyes. It was this man's quick thinking that allowed the speed of the beast to be reduced to a progressive halt, so that he was then able to throw himself across the seat and fully pull up the handbrake to make us safe once again. Our saviour was obviously as badly shaken as we were, if not worse, and had he considered giving David a right thrashing there and then, his reaction would have been completely justified, and probably even applauded by me and Chris.

But instead, he simply dragged David out of the car by the seat of his pants, tucked him under his arm and with the little rascal shouting, writhing, and thrashing out in all directions, simply carried him into the factory and handed him back to Mum and Dad in the hope that any punishment administered would be one David would remember for a long, long, time to come.

However, this is another case where none of us can remember what his punishment was.

Why is it that with a little help from my siblings I am able to give a reasonably accurate narrative of each event as it took place? However, what is bemusing is I cannot ever seem to recall what occurred after the event and as a result each statement falls flat due to its abrupt finish.

It would be so good if I were able to describe the thoughts that went through our minds before undertaking these ridiculous escapades and then augment these with those of Dad's chastising lectures after the event, add in the punishment we received, if any, and if there was ever any improvement in our behaviour albeit just short-term.

What is certain is that no penalty ever seemed to make any difference, we just carried on doing untold mischief over and over again, which is a fact I am sure you will by now quite willingly endorse. As regretful as it is, there is nothing I can now do about our behaviour as it was then, hence I had better just move on to the next tale.

While we are talking about behaviour, I have to tell you about a visit to my Grandparents in Wood Green North London. This must have been on a visit to London and probably around the time of the David *driving lesson* incident.

We were all dressed up in our Sunday best and Mum seemed to be on edge that day and fussing over us throughout our journey to ensure we remained pristine, not an easy feat where David is concerned. Upon arrival to their house, I have a very vivid recollection of us being placed side by side in the hall next to the grandfather clock where we stood like guardsmen on sentry duty.

Mum like any self-respecting sergeant major, gave us one final inspection, buttoning up our coats, straightening our ties and repeated her declaration that on pain of death, we must remember our manners, be on our absolute best behaviour, and make her proud.

What I need to make clear at this point is that my grandfather, Christian, had come to the UK from Germany with his wife, my Dutch Grandmother Julia when they were young. Grandad had worked hard and made his way up to become managing director of a company making buttons, of the *sew on your coat* type.

My Dad had been the general manager in control of the production and ensuring all the various machines were correctly set and maintained. This is where he met my mum a machine hand at the same factory. Grandad was not at all happy with this association and did his best to dissuade his son from carrying on with it.

Dad would not listen to his father, pleading that the courtship had been going on longer than his father was aware and that it was true love. Grandad was not happy to hear he had been deceived and continued to air his displeasure, so much so that when they arranged to get married he actually brutally and unswervingly sacked them both on the spot.

Given this trauma, you can understand why it was especially important for my Mum to show that she had bought up her boys to be a great example to their loving parents guidance. I believe she hoped that our paternal Grandfather would be able to recognise our mother and fathers' achievements should we be granted a chance to meet with them and give a hope that his might lead to a reconciliation.

That said, I have to add that Nanny Mayer was not of that ilk at all and was an absolutely adorable lady that loved Mum and us to bits, as did Auntie Julie.

When Grandad finally condescended to grant us this audience Nanny told us, when invited in we should stand with our backs to the sideboard in the lounge. Once we had been fully versed in our duties by both mum and Nanny, we were trooped in and followed our instructions to the letter.

Nanny then stepped back and stood with her back to the door like an attentive servant. The invitation had not been extended to Mum, not that she would have taken up the invite, so we were on our own for this one.

There we faced Grandad who was sitting in the bay window, dressed in his Sunday best with full suit, waistcoat, and tie. With his gold watch chain in place between his waistcoat buttonhole and pocket, he was sitting in his big plush navy-blue leather swing chair and displaying an air of total authority reminiscent of a high court judge about to pass sentence.

I was terrified and stood there quaking in my boots hoping he would not speak to me directly. But he asked each of us questions in turn and when it came to my turn, I replied in a very timid quiet voice. He then boomed *"speak up boy"* which startled me and with a quivering voice I repeated my reply a little louder, while at the same time thinking, why did he call me boy surely he knows my name? The interview, as I recall it, was very brief and Grandad soon gestured with a wave of the hand for us to leave.

Nanny Mayer then opened the drawer of the sideboard and handed us each a Fry's Chocolate Cream bar (I have no idea where they came from?) and without a further prompt we remembered our manners impeccably, thanked them both, bid our goodbyes and left the room.

Once we were back in the hall, I burst into tears, Nanny immediately stooped to hold me in her arms and said *"Vos a masser micher"* – *"What is the matter with you"* in English but with her Dutch accent.

Then realising I had found Grandad a bit overbearing she then led me by the hand into the front parlour and with the others following, sat down in her favourite armchair. With me close beside her she took my chocolate bar unwrapped it and after handing it back gave me a big cuddle. In the meantime, David with delight in his eyes, was best part of the way into finishing his, and Chris was not far behind.

That is the singular recollection I have of my

paternal Grandfather. Remember I was only four when we left London and if there were any earlier meetings with him before that, they are no longer part of my memory bank.

He died when I was seven years old, so it looks likely that this visit was our last and possibly David and my one and only meeting. Mum said that was the one and only time that she entered the house after the family rift and as soon as she ensured we were presentable, she immediately went to wait in the street.

I believe the meeting was brokered by Auntie Julie in an attempt to reunite the family, or at least bring the children into the fold.

I believe Dad was even more resolute and never saw his dad alive again after he moved out of the family house. He did keep in touch with the remainder of his family and met with them on neutral ground from time to time and as I have already shown his mother and sister were willing to go against Grandads wishes.

Returning to the Norfolk phase of our lives Dad was now out of work, broke and with a wife and three growing lads to feed, needed work, any work, any work that is, that paid reasonably and promptly.

A bungalow was being built on a derelict piece of land opposite our house and he started there as a labourer, digging trenches for the footings, mixing cement, pre-cement mixers, so by hand, and manually carting bricks, joists, rafters, and the like around the site until the bungalow was complete and there he was out of work again.

For a short time, he worked at the docks repairing the mechanical equipment of the ships, but this work was only available when the shipyard had suitable work. Sometimes he would work there on a ship when it was being repaired in the dry dock. A dry dock is where they float the ship into the dock, close some great big doors behind it and then pump out all the water and as they do so they hastily install a large number of wooden poles as wedges between the dock wall and the side of the ship to support it and stop it toppling over.

Once all the water had been pumped out, the ship then sat upright in the empty dry dock being held in place by the supports. With possible ten of the fifteen metres of its height all covered in limpets, barnacles and other crustations below its now exposed waterline the ships would look quite forlorn. Before work commenced a series of planks were then laid on top of these poles at various levels to act as walkways, with rope as railings and ladders.to allow access at various levels.

On this particular day he went off to work at the docks and arrived home very soon after, looking as white as a sheet and trembling all over.

It seems that he had been carrying an armful of tools while climbing onto one of the walkways and the plank he stepped onto was not secured and slipped under him. He lost his balance, tottered, fell over the edge and plunged towards the hard concrete base of the dock many metres below, but managed to thrust out an arm and grab hold of one of the support poles a few metres below where he had fallen.

There he was dangling there will his legs desperately flapping about as he summoned all his bodily strength and hauled himself onto the pole where he clung on for dear life with the sound of his tools clanging onto the concrete far below and echoing all around the dock. However, it was not yet his lucky day because the walkway above him was too high to reach and the one below was a long, long, way down and not directly below him anyway.

He said that he was laying on the pole with his arms folded round it desperately trying not to lose grip, but nevertheless knew that he needed to move to a safer position if there was such a thing, given his predicament. He then realised that if he positioned himself over the walkway well to his right, albeit a long way down, if he fell it would at least break his fall and give him a chance to grab the railing rope or something to hold onto. He said he gingerly slid himself along the pole until he reached the dock wall, and it was only then that he realised that some of his workmates were calling to him to offer advice, his concentration and fear having blocked them out until then.

Apparently the guys all rallied round and got themselves organised with some ladders which they quickly lowered down to where he was and he gingerly edged his way up. After a strong cup of tea with lots of sugar he thanked everyone for their help, got on a bus and came home never to return again.

Dad had, in between getting normal paid jobs, worked with a local scrap metal dealer dismantling now redundant wartime military vehicles and aircraft that were then abundantly available.

He got paid a percentage of the scrap metal value of the items he manually disassembled, but this meant breaking every item down to it raw metal origin.

This was generally a long laborious process, especially as there was no mechanised assistance like electric screwdrivers. Mind you everything was scrap so a lot of it was broken apart by hammer and chisel, because it was never going to be of any further use.

To assist him Dad did make a number of jigs to hold items in place while he hit them with the hammer to split one metal from the next.

It was when dissembling one of these pieces of scrap aircraft component, namely a uniselector which it basically a switch that can turn on or off a large number of items at once, that he hit a minor jackpot.

Breaking these into their raw components became far more lucrative than the norm because the main component was the switch and each switch lever had minute little contacts made of platinum.

In this case Dad took a percentage from the scrap dealer for the switch lever parts but went straight to a jeweller for a hundred percent payment plan for the platinum metal contacts.

Each contact may have been minute and just a miniscule part of each uniselector, but he did say that these tiny pieces of platinum not much bigger than a grain of sugar paid five hundred times more per item of weight than any of the other metal did.

I think this little windfall helped to keep their heads above water during this very precarious time in our lives.

Not that any of us children noticed any difference to our exceptionally cosseted lives.

Having spent the previous five or six years as a self-employed engineer it was becoming increasingly difficult to maintain a regular income and Dad decided to bite the bullet and take a fulltime job somewhere.

Scanning the situations vacant sections of the local newspapers he eventually came across a job vacancy at the company Laurence-Scott Electro-Motors Ltd. in Norwich, advertised in the in the Gt. Yarmouth Mercury which he applied for. He was offered the position and decided to take it.

Although this should have been a lifeline for us at the time, I have to say this job became one that he eventually grew to hate with a passion.

The reasons were manyfold but among them was that the work was for production line assembly of small components like precision sliders for the viewfinders on army tanks.

He said that the work was just repetitively assembling the same item day after day and this was somewhat an insult to his abilities. When he discovered what it was he was making, he found it very difficult to understand why they were needed, because not so very long ago he had been breaking up very similar items for scrap. It seems that the company was still manufacturing many items for the military although by then the war had been finished some five or six years.

Certain components they manufactured, although similar, were upgraded versions or new designs to the ones familiar to Dad. The military had retained a great deal of the wartime equipment to allow them to be battle ready and the new items were part of the ongoing need to replace a proportion of the stock with the latest versions. At least that's how Dad explained it to me many years later.

His main regret with the work there was that it was piece work. That is, you had a target figure to achieve each day and everything above that earned you a bonus payment. Why should he be against the chance to earn more money? Well, in truth, at the start he wasn't, but as things progressed earning became increasingly more difficult.

Initially he was incredibly pleased with this deal, because he could earn good wages. But it was not long before it got him into some deep water. Like most repetitive jobs the longer you were carrying out the exact same task to complete, the more competent you became, and with that came the ability to finish it faster, and Dad became amazingly fast.

This upset the majority of his work colleagues because they wanted to plod along at a steady pace in the belief that if they completed the tasks any quicker the bonus rate would have been reviewed.

These guys would often have extended tea breaks and long sessions of discussion where no work got done. Dad's thoughts were that he was there for the money and considered the indolent workforce to be just swinging the lead. Because these protocols were totally alien to Dad's personal work ethic, he carried on completing the tasks in an accurate and speedy manner despite their objections.

His work colleagues then conspired to force a change by convincing his supervisors to shift him to a new task as soon as he was able to get up to a good bonus speed with the current one.

That meant he would drop to the bottom of the learning curve, and it would take time to get to earn minimum bonus once again.

Undeterred, he tried to accept the workers manipulation of the totally spineless management, bear the constant hostility from his co-workers, as well as the enforced exclusion from every one of their daily conversations. For some considerable time, he took all this with a stiff upper lip, and grudgingly took this on the chin, which he saw as part of his duty to his family.

Mum did mention to me many years later, that for ages, when he came home she would ask how his day had gone and he would just smile and said they are still being pathetic.

However, in the end it was probably more the drop in earnings, that made him see that it was a lost cause, so he eventually and reluctantly threw in the towel and unwillingly went back to earning a living by smashing up ex-military equipment in order to turn it back into virgin metal once again.

Another chapter in our life began, and this could have been prior to, during or after Lawrence Scott, Mum and Dad had been busy changing our property into a boarding house. Like an Airbnb but using very crude marketing methods and zero technology.

To this end Mum and Dad, and us children as well, gave up our bedrooms to make this possible.

From having a bedroom each, us boys were now set up all together in one of the reception rooms at the front, which had previously been Dad's work room, but was now our highly condensed personal space and communal bedroom.

Mum and Dad then slept in the kitchen. The other two reception rooms were then used as the dining room and lounge area.

To ensure the accommodation remained in pristine condition us children were totally banned from going upstairs for any reason, not even to use the bathroom.

As a result, the kitchen sink became our bathroom where we would have to get bathed and washed. We were also limited to the toilet facilities provided by the ground floor toilet in the lobby just outside the kitchen.

In fact, this arrangement immediately reminds me of an incident when I was probably about nine years old which I can vividly recall.

With the bathroom out of bounds, Mum had filled the kitchen sink with hot water, lifted me in, given me a bar of soap and a flannel and left me to wash myself all over. There I was busily doing my ablutions as instructed and turned round, where to my horror staring in at the window were the daughters of two of the guests, Jill and her sister Andria. There they were gawking wide eyed at me as I stood there stark naked with just a face flannel to save my dignity.

Initially I just froze, then not sure whether to show my bum or be brash, cover my other profile with the flannel and nonchalantly stare them out.

I elected to turn away, use the flannel to screen my posterior, then screamed at the top of my voice for Mum, who came running thinking I had severely injured myself. She was mightily relieved and highly amused to find that the only thing I was suffering from was my loss of self-respect. In any case, they both scarpered the moment I let out my holler.

I should say Jill was about ten and Andria about my age and although they had no brothers, I'm still bemused as to why my scrawny skeletal little body could have possibly been of any great interest to them because there was very little of me to see anyway!!

Mum was quite unperturbed by the whole episode and thought it quite funny, so much so that Mum relayed this event to their parents who also thought it hilarious, whereas I was totally devastated and highly embarrassed by the event and even more so by the gossip. There was worse to come because both girls became perpetual nuisances by hanging around me like limpets for the remainder of their stay and continually hounded me to play kiss chase. Ugg!

It looks like David was in the wrong age ballpark for them and as such avoided their amorous advances.

Or maybe he just explained in the simplest terms what would happen if they tried it on with him!

Their parents liked a bit of a tipple so after giving the girls a brief trip to the beach each day, they would leave them with their hosts, us, and nip to the pub on the corner before dinner – and after too!

God was I pleased when they left to go home to London. But they still had the last laugh by insisting on smothering me with hugs and big kisses in front of everyone including my brothers as they finally left to go home.

Obviously, this was of great amusement to my family and started a bout of perpetual teasing from both my brothers, which continued for a long time after.

Despite Chris and David's mocking, I did manage to up my game sufficiently to become a minor hero to one female during the boarding house era.

One of our tiny visitors, a little girl of about four years old had gone to the bathroom and locked the door but couldn't open it again. She was very distraught, crying out for mummy and needed someone to rescue her. Dad had press ganged me into carrying out this feat of skill, ingenuity and daring. I quickly pulling on my 'S' emblazoned y-fronts over my shorts and was ready for the challenge.

OK you know that's a lie. What I actually did was look at Dad incredulously and say *"You want me to do what! – please tell me you are joking!"* or similar protests.

To me this sounded more like a job for the SAS, and he would be better off calling in the self-trained master of such daring – David. However, obviously Dad had decided this was the day that his wimp of a son was going to be made to man up. No argument he was going to have to do it or die in the attempt.

Dad had come to seek me out while I was playing it the back garden. I then followed him to the front garden where he had already placed a ladder up against the roof of the porch in an attempt to reach the open bathroom window.

However, even with the ladder angled as much as he dared there was still a gap of about a metre between the ladder and the open window.

The plan was for me to go up to the very top of the ladder with Dad close behind me and while he supported me as best he could, I was to attempt to bridge the gap somehow, someway, anyhow - just do it son.

I was absolutely terrified and needed a great deal of coaxing and encouragement to even attempt this feat. It was getting to the point where Dad was becoming exasperated at my failure to even try it.

In the meantime, the captive little child's pleas sounded increasingly more desperate, so I bit the bullet and attempted to leap across the gap. I did manage to get my foot onto the window ledge but overbalanced, tottered lost my footing and plunged downward.

Mum screamed, but Dad was still hanging onto one of my arms and in any case I would only have fallen onto the porch roof and providing I didn't roll off, would have lived for another attempt.

Mum's pleading to just break the bathroom door down fell on deaf ears. Dad decided that new doors cost money and wimps can generally be repaired cheaply, or discarded, so I was not given any other choice but to attempt again.

Mum fearing the worse, could not bear to look at another effort and ran inside. Before I had a chance to protest Dad scooped me up and using all his strength just launched me at the open window feet first.

It worked because one third of me was in and two thirds out, and with two hands supporting me on the windowsill below.

I was unable to move otherwise I would have totally fallen out. Dad, hollered to Mum to come and help, which she immediately obliged thinking that she was going to find me in a number of pieces all over the front path. He got her to fetch a broom which he then got me to grab hold of and he used it to help lift me up so that I could slide in backward on top of the bathroom sink.

When I got down I saw that the little girl was curled into a ball and with her hands pulled up close to and covering her face she seemed totally stressed.

I slid back the bolt and bent down and took her hand, saying *"its open, lets go"* but it was still some time before it registered with her. When she was able to loose her fear and move, I was able to open the door and let her out. Her mum swept her into her arms and her dad then thrust out both arms and cuddled the pair of them.

Dad arrived almost immediately and gave me the usual ruffle of my hair, and a *"well done son — It wasn't so bad was it."* I'm not so sure I agreed, but at least her mum and dad also gave me a cuddle in appreciation so overall I was very pleased and exhilarated by having finally achieved a daring task at least once in my life.

I only wished my brothers had been there to witness that I too could complete the impossible.

Sorry, I digressed yet again. Going back a page or two I need to say now the one or two of the houses opposite and along from us a bit were also set up as boarding houses, which I think gave my parents the original idea to convert ours too. As I remember it Mum had long discussions with one of the ladies that ran one of these. It is from these little chats that she learned the does and don'ts, as well as most importantly, what to charge.

Obviously with no internet, Google or any of the media methods available today, another affordable means of advertising was needed. The answer was to send letters to everyone she knew in London letting them know she was open for business. Telephones were a highly expensive luxury that unlike the garage we could not afford, and besides this the thought of talking to someone via one would put most normal people into a sweat.

Bookings likewise to the advertising, were also done by the highly inefficient and error probable method of sending letters back and forth.

As you can imagine writing and sending out *we're open for business* letters in January, showing the dates available meant at best a *'booking'* might not be made for a couple of weeks while people thought about it.

And then others would *'book'* only to find that someone had pipped them to the post for those dates and further letters were needed. Another difficulty was that this was an era when we were a totally cash society. Everyone received their wages in banknotes and coins, and they likewise paid out everything in the same manner. A booking could only be accepted if the deposit had been received by registered post and a confirmation letter had been sent to the guests, again by registered mail. This somewhat archaic method of booking a holiday was as I said, error probable.

Such, that on more than one occasion people turned up for their holidays believing they had made a booking when clearly they had not, because no cash had arrived by registered post, and they could not show the receipt.

Sadly, in one case, a mother arrived with her three children leaving her husband at home because he *felt unwell* on the day. It transpired that he was the one supposed to post the registered letter with the booking deposit many months earlier.

But instead, he used the money to bet on a tip a good friend told him was dead cert' winning horse and of course it lost!

He was then too afraid to tell the family about what he had done and on the travel day faked illness instead of facing the music. Sad but true.

All that said, generally speaking, Jill and family apart, we enjoyed having the visitors here and very often we would receive a parting gift from them in gratitude as they reluctantly left for home.

For those of you that think that the lack of recent comment meant that Dave had reformed his character, and there are no other incidents I can relay, I am sorry to disappoint, because I am about to recall another escapade. I am not sure how or why, but David was given some little animals in a cage. It could be that maybe someone else had been told to dispose of them and David being a lover of all animals willingly accepted them as pets. Whatever the reason David acquired these white mice in a cage. My recollection is that the mice and the cage were banned from the house by mum and ended up living outside in the lean-too.

What is true is that Mum was not enamoured with the idea of having these creatures in her house at all, no more than I was either. However, David and that meant Dad too, thought they were cute little beings. David would often take them out of the cage and let them run up his arms, across his shoulders and inside his shirt, which used to make me shiver to think of this and worse to see him do it.

On the day in question the guests were in the middle of having dinner and Mum had asked me to take a jug of water in and place it in the middle of the dining table, which I had just done. I then noticed David had the three mice running all over him and for whatever reason had decided to bring them into the dining room to show to everybody.

Despite me trying to shoo him away, he did manage to get right up the side of a lady sitting at the dinner table and say, *"how do you like my mice."*

224

The very obvious result that she leapt up from the table and in so doing, sent her chair, dinner, and most of the items on the table including the jug of water flying in all directions whilst screaming many obscenities at him, which even his young ears could not have failed to translate as *"can you please remove them this instant."* The action was loudly endorsed by the other ladies and most of the men too as the situation became even more chaotic.

To make matters even worse her husband as well as joining in the kerfuffle, tried to forcibly remove David from the room with the result that he lost control of the mice and they took their chance of freedom by two leaping onto the table and one onto the floor.

Obviously, the uproar in the dining room attracted Mum and Dad to the crisis in seconds only to be confronted with great deal of foul language and threatened murder going on. They then did their absolute best to calm the situation.

Firstly, by offering them a noose to put round David's neck. Then by Dad diving into his back pocket to produce a mediating offer of cash which 'the guests' willingly accepted and immediately made a beeline for the pub on the corner. With the mice now free to run anywhere, the need to capture them became the priority. Mum and I chose to bow out of this one because we believed that the best tool for capture might be just a twelve-bore shotgun.

At around the pub closing time a highly inebriated noisy set of what then could only very loosely be described as our *guests,* returned all fired up and eager to carry out the delayed lynching.

However, Dad instead calmly fed them a complete pack of lies that convinced them the mice had been successfully recaptured, although in reality, despite an extensive search only one mouse had been re-interned in its cage.

But when thankfully they finally departed a few days later, just to avoid any later repercussions, mum substantially reduced the bill as a sweetener.

When Dad heard of this he was annoyed with what he considered was a totally unnecessary peace offering, stating that for their attitude when they returned from the pub, he would have willingly cast them out in the street that night with their belongings following them, and without any compensation.

It is at this point that I really do have to say that mice aside, my younger brother David from infant though to now has been a character cherished by almost everyone he meets and adored by more than a few. He is amiable, witty, a full of fun guy without any airs and graces. He is also a very caring person, always the first to offer help, not afraid to get his hands dirty and willing to go where others fear to tread.

My hero and dearly loved brother.

David, can I have your thanks in cash please!

Running a boarding house in the UK provided my parents with an annual short-term income window. Although we longed for the visitors to leave so that we could have our own beds back, no sooner had the summer guests left us than the fishing fleets arrived. They would start to appear in October and usually stay until the end of November. The arrival of the fishing fleet was an annual occurrence determined by the movement of the shoals of herring off the coast. The fleet followed these fish as the seasonal weather pattens drove them south toward warmer waters as winter approached

There were always home-based fishing boats that left and returned to Gt. Yarmouth each day and landed a variety of fish. However, when the *season* arrived it bought with it an extra hundred and fifty to two hundred ships, there to specifically catch herring.

OK so they provided additional much needed income for our family, but even then at our ages it was difficult to see that forgoing a comfortable bed was a preferable alternative to eating bread and lard.

The wives of the fishing boat crews would follow their husbands from port to port as the trawlers followed the migration of the fish to warmer waters.

They lodged in boarding houses like ours during their time there following the work. The husbands would join them for the short periods of leave they got.

The majority of the crew were Scottish and as such us children had great difficulty understanding anything they said. I can remember that if they spoke to me I just stood there staring at them blankly and they would repeat it a number of times, before adding *"weits oop we ye laddy de ye no inderstind English"* and walk away shaking their head. Chris claims he could understand them perfectly and would decipher for the rest of the family. I'm not sure why they bothered to ask me then!

The women generally worked long hours at the fish market gutting and cleaning the fish as soon as they were landed and as a result we rarely saw them either.

One of the products that Great Yarmouth was famous for was bloaters. These are herrings that have been cold smoked over oak in brick kiln ovens in the traditional way. A bloater is a less salty and has a less intense flavour to its cousin the kipper. The curing, packing and shipping of these delicacies was a major industry in Great Yarmouth and their output dwarfed that of the other East Anglia coastal towns that also produced them. I myself can remember the smoke houses in South Denes where the herring were smoked to preserve them, after which they became bloaters.

Chris has got a good knowledge and recollection of the Trawlers, the Scottish fishing people, and the related industry that went into full production mode during those few months.

In fact, during these periods him and *Jacques* would disappear for hours and be down by the quayside watching the trawlers coming and going along the river to deliver their catch and then turn round, go to sea and do it all again. By hanging around the fish market they would scrounge fish from the fisher women then run string through the gills and mouth to make a string to enable them to carry the fish home. Quite often the women would also arrive home with fish, so that there were far to many for the family and visitors to eat. Chris would then rush off and try to sell the extra ones.

One of the places for possible custom for him was the Greyhound pub on the corner. One thing is for certain, with his gift of the gab no fish ended up in the bin. While on the subject of Chris's money-making schemes, he also chopped and sold firewood as well as collect coke from the gas works on a Saturday and sold that on too.

He had to collect wooden packing cases and pallets, break them down to the bare wood, then saw it into short lengths. He would then use an axe to chop the wood into kindle then string it into small bundles and tout it around the neighbourhood. He later found it was easier to sell the bundles in bulk to Wragg's the grocers as well as Willis's greengrocer opposite us.

This was in the days when the main way to heat the home was with coal, coke or logs in an open hearth. Gas for cooking was produced locally by the Gas Board. This was the result of heating coal in giant ovens to make coal gas, which was then piped to customers to burn for illumination, heating, and cooking. Once all the gas had been extracted from the coal it was sold off as coke. Chris could collect the coke from the 'back door' of the Gas Works in a wheelbarrow, and at home bag it up into potato sacks he had obtained from the greengrocer. He then loaded the heavy sacks into the wheelbarrow and went off to shop it around the neighbourhood. He had quite a number of regular customers eager to put it on the fire.

As I have intimated a number of times, the day to day running of even a small guest house requires a lot of graft, and a much greater workload than can be carried out by one person.

Obviously there were meals to cook, beds to change and wash as well as keeping the house spic and span, so Mum needed help. To assist with this, just before each holiday season commenced mum would arrange for Nanny Gast, Mum's Mum, to come up by coach from London to help her with the day-to-day chores.

Sometime around the beginning of May each year we would be at the bus stop along Southtown Road eagerly waiting for her to arrive on a Grey-Green coach from London. This was an arduous journey of between eight to ten hours, with a few essential stops along the way to allow the passengers to 'become comfortable' before spending a few more hours seated and all cooped up. Nan did try to carry out the journey by train once but because of the vast number of platforms, the need to keep asking 'which train', and then having to read all the station names to ensure she got off at the correct one, she was unable to relax and enjoy the experience so she said "never again."

We would sit on the bench by the bus-stop, all excited and expectantly awaiting her arrival.

There were times I can remember, which I assume must have been when guest numbers were low, so probably early or late season, that more time was available to take us out. We would get back from school, wash our hands and faces and tidy ourselves up, and off we would go. Nan would then take us for a walk and along the way buy us an ice-cream, if the shop had any that is - We were still on rationing, remember, so if we did get one it was a highly special day.

Another great reminisce of mine is the day Nan took us to Gorleston by open topped bus. We got to play on the beach, have a picnic there, demolish an ice-cream and finish it off the day with a return trip on the open top bus again. A fantastic day with our beloved Nan. I think this must have been towards the end of the season and possibly our treat from Nan just before she returned to London. We really enjoyed having Nanny there because she would pamper and dote upon us at every possible moment throughout her stay. Her close attention to ensure we were always happy and smiling showed in the loved she radiated towards us. We three were equally as loving in return and were always sad when it came time for her to leave again to London. The mood was very sombre while we sat on the bench waiting for the coach to arrive. It was a very emotional scene because Nan would give mum and all three of us in turn round after round of hugs while we were waiting. After embracing each of us, she would only need to glance in our direction for it to compel her to give us all another cuddle and this continued until the coach arrived and she was off to ensure our cousins got their share of this unending love. The silly thing is that neither David nor I can recall Chris being on any trips with Nanny Gast, but I am sure he was included.

It was somewhere towards the latter period of the Gt. Yarmouth era that David and I became more alert to adult conversations and began earwigging between Mum and Dad's discussions, or Mum and neighbours and slowly it became apparent to us that we were going to have another brother or God forbid a sister.

Thus, being unaware of what a gooseberry looked like, and even worse having no clue as to what a bush full of them looked like, we spent a lot of time looking under each likely contender, without finding any real clues. Then we heard one lady ask when the stork might arrive, and it was then obvious we had been given a bum steer, so from thereon we spent our time staring up at the rooftops. That is the strange thing, our parents never sat us down and told us that the family was about to be extended. David and I just got the odd snippet of information from gossip and put two and two together. We never even talked it over with Chris.

I think their reluctance to tell us was that it was quite late in their lives for them to be increasing their family and as such the risk of the pregnancy not going full term was, in them days, reasonably high. Thus, it was better not to raise our hopes, only to have to dash them later.

On Friday June 13th 1952, Mum was missing which was a very unusual occurrence. Nanny Gast was charged with looking after us for most of the day, whilst at the same time attempting to ward off an inquisition from us children concerned for their mum's absence.

Sometime in the late afternoon Dad arrived home in a very cheery mood and carrying a number of small ice cream blocks all tightly wrapped up in newspaper to stop them from melting, together with a bottle of Corona ice-cream soda.

Both of which were another rarity in the late 1940s. *"I have a big surprise that I need to tell you about and to celebrate, we are going to have ice cream sodas."*

He then grabbed some glass tumblers dropped an ice cream block in each and filled them to the top with the cream soda and the whole concoction then began to fizz and foam.

Once we all had our fizzy cream drinks in front of us he announced *"Well, boys I have just returned from seeing Mum in hospital . . . . ,"* The word Hospital hit me like a ton of bricks, and immediate visions of injury or worse sprung to mind, *". . . . . and I am delighted to tell you that you have a baby sister called Anne Julia Louise."*

My heart started to beat again and this time with the sheer delight that we now had our own baby sister. It seemed that David and I were correct all along in believing a new baby was on its way, but well off the right track with our thoughts of gooseberry bushes and storks, hence it was a complete shock to find hospital was the delivery method we were not anticipating. So much for eavesdropping as an intelligence gathering technique! Meanwhile, although we were enjoying the pleasure provided by our cool summer drink, we were overjoyed, but nevertheless swamped Dad with lots of questions and became increasingly more exuberant and animated by the whole idea of the addition of a girl to our family.

I am not sure how long Mum was in hospital, be it a day or more, her return was a moment that changed our lives forever.

We were all thrilled to see our beautiful baby sister and gathered round to make gooey noises, blow raspberries and other nonsense sounds in an attempt to communicate with her in baby parlance, but despite out combined efforts smiles were not forthcoming.

It was very soon after her homecoming that we realised she had bought with her a totally incurable contagious disease called insomnia, that she then made absolutely sure she passed on to all of us.

I could only recall one previous instance of being awoken in the night by a noise. That noise was so severe that I was frightened by it. I recall laying there trying to determine what it could be as I became more and more terrified. I then convinced myself it was probably a big grizzly bear or equally monstrous beast making this ear shattering sound as it devoured the rest of my family. I screamed for Dad. Such was my level of distress that he immediately leapt out of bed, and instantly the noise stopped – It was him that had been the snoring grizzly bear!

Being continually woken in the night by this new arrival meant that the novelty of having a baby sister soon wore off. Our previous delight was further dampened because Anne could also vent her displeasure during the day for no discernible reason. This meant us having to take it in turns to rock the pram or cot in a futile attempt to lull her to sleep, severely impeding our own reign of terror.

Even when this did work, the effects were very

short lived because she would be bawling again within a few minutes.

Mum would be at her wits end at times and would ask us to take Anne for a walk in her pram out of earshot to see if she would go to sleep.

Invariably this meant us pushing the pram to the farthest corner of the field and leaving her to cry while we went off to play elsewhere.

This quite often did actually work, because after a few hours of screaming at the top of her lungs she would be so exhausted she would go into a coma.

Actually, now I think about it, by parking the pram next to *Drake the snakes* wall, we were actually giving him payback for the times he grassed us up! Upon hearing the din I'm sure customers would have wanted to be in and out of the shop as soon as possible, thereby disrupting the daily gossip between butcher and shopper. Result!!

Having now introduced Anne into our life story, I am sorry but other than her incessant screaming there is not much that I can add about her life at this stage.

But this is a good reason for you to buy the next book in the series.

I have to ask if I told you I also have a brother called Chris? I'll forgive you if you have forgotten him and my apologies for allowing you to believe he was just a figment of your imagination.

He does exist and we must give him full marks for being wise enough to ensure most of his exploits were events carried out beyond the sight of his brother John, who would otherwise have undoubtedly enlightened you to all of his misdemeanours in this book. Honestly, it is not that I have any good reason to shut him out of my early life or that he was simply a very well-behaved child, which he certainly was not. The main reason the overall content of this tome ignores him completely is just that whatever he did do, he very successfully hid from me and the rest of the world.

Anyway, the next tale does actually feature Chris, oh, and of course David. On the day in question, I understand Chris asked Mum if he and his school friend *Jacques* could take us to the playing fields locally. Chris and *Jacques* were about thirteen years old by then, so obviously mature enough to take care of his younger brothers.

Nonetheless, it seems Mum was very apprehensive to start with, but then Jacques assured her that he wouldn't leave our sides. Mum thought highly of Jacques, so after some deliberation and persuasion she relented. We were given a whole load of doe's and don'ts including instructions to stick together no matter what.

With our directives firmly implanted in our minds and without any further hesitation we were off with our minders to keep us in check. But, with previous promises already forgotten we were not going anywhere near the playing field, but for a walk by the river instead.

Can you already see where this is going to end up?

I can no longer remember whose decision it was to go to the river, but whoever offered the choice it was willingly accepted by all.

Without further thought we had soon walked past the fire station turned into Ferry Lane and were down by the quayside in minutes.

Initially we were simply happy to walk along looking at the ships, well, that was until Chris decided to jump on one of a ship mooring ropes, which made it vibrate up and down and make a deep humming sound.

It seemed such fun that we all then jumped on every rope of every ship we passed.

That is until a seaman hollered at us from the deck and in return got a cheeky reply. He immediately leapt up and was on his way down the gangplank in a flash, so we had to run as fast as our little legs could carry us.

Fortunately, he soon gave up and instead vented some seaman's salty phrases in our direction in an enraged attempt to dissuade us from continuing this annoying game.

Once we were sure the old seadog had given up we slowed our pace, took time to catch our breath and make a mental note of the new words we had just learnt, before again getting up to any new antics.

It was not long before we were passing the Trinity House storage area where they store the supplies for Lighthouses, moor Lighthouse Ships in for repair, and maintain the marker buoys.

We noticed the security gate was open and saw that a couple of the buoys had the access hatch open.

There appeared to be nobody around, so we decided to creep into the area.

I say *we* but I mean - Chris, David and Jacques. I was too cowardly to enter because it looked to me like trouble if you stepped past the perimeter fence.

They took a look inside the open ones, only to find they were just rusty and smelly steel vessels with nothing of any interest inside them at all, but they did make a wonderful echo when you yodelled inside one of them. The tribe then took it in turns to bellow at the top of their voices and thought this was great fun to hear the echo all over the harbour.

That was until a security man in uniform shouted back from just behind them *"What do you think you are doing"* which made them jump out of their skins.

This guardian of these two-ton pieces of rusty old junk had quietly slunk out from behind a row of them, crept up to the hooligans and was now blocking their escape. They knew there was no way out of this, so when instructed meekly fell in line and followed him towards their impending fate.

A second security guard then appeared from the back of the gate house and selected a key from an enormous bunch, unlocked the security office door and went in. Calling in the troops to assist with this minor intrusion onto private property seemed well OTT but upon reflection it was trespass onto Crown Property with the obvious highly serious penalties.

I was not sure whether to take the sensible option, turn on my heels and scarper sharpish leaving them to face the music, or stride forward and insist their legal rights were upheld. I did neither and just hid behind the corner of the next building and watched things unfold from afar.

With the pitiful little group being escorted to their final fate, I peered cautiously from my observation point imagining that the guard inside was likely to be attaching shackles to the wall hooks to make it ready for these reprobates to be slapped in irons and left to rot away in there. Once again it would be me unfairly left to explain to Mum and Dad why they should not expect them back any time soon or maybe never again.

As soon as the captives arrived at the guard house their custodian stood before them and gave a lecture which was beyond my earshot. He then lined them up by a wall, which worried me because it looked very much like he was about to assemble a firing squad.

Much to my relief, he instead pointed to a notice on the other wall, and they all stood there staring at it for some time. It then dawned on me that they were reading the rules and regulations for access to the site, and I thought maybe it was a bit late in the day for them to be learning these lessons. Then with a wave of his arm they were dismissed and sent on their way by their would-be captors.

They then gladly ran off to seek me out, give me a lot of grief for my cowardice and for not being there to take the rap with them. I must ask, why would I want to get involved in this petty criminality when anyone with an ounce of common sense could tell it would be very foolhardy?

With them continuing to question why I lacked the normal brotherly allegiance siblings can expect from each other, I sauntered along at the back of the group feeling miserable and dejected.

It seemed to me that Chris and Jacques were regretting ever suggesting taking us with them on their capers. I had to agreed too and wished I had been left at home, because we had done nothing but get into trouble since the moment we left home. All we had done since setting out was to go from one mischievous exploit to the next despite it being obvious that it would annoy other people.

We then carried on along by the quayside, walking toward Gorleston, with the rascals in our group picking up stones or anything that looked like it was discarded, and hurling it as far out into the river as they could.

Having found a suitable missile, they would stand well back from the quayside and then in order to give them momentum run as fast as they could towards the river edge and release the item at the very last moment.

Although David was half of Chris and Jacques age at the time he was still able to gain an impressive distance with his throws but frightened me to death because a lot of his runs stopped awfully close to the waters' edge.

Despite their promises to Mum neither Chris nor Jacques ever seemed to see how quickly fun could change to become a harrowing disaster.

They never thought about what would happen if one fell in or if there were any small boats passing as they hurled things into the water.

The quayside was a sheer drop to the water some five metres below with no means whatsoever of being able to scale the sides to save themselves. One little stumble or slip and it was certain death. As you will see if you look at the ferry photograph.

Even though the older two could probably swim, the river currents would have made it impossible for them to stay afloat long enough to be rescued. Despite my continual protestations safety continued to be ignored, and these were instead countered with threats of me being one of the missiles if I didn't shut up. So, I shut up! We carried on causing havoc along the quayside, generally because the others were still throwing things into the water.

The ships were generally moored stern to aft with only a very little gap between the hulls, such that if their aim was off the mark they would end up hitting the hull of one or the other of the ships, which made a clang and vibrate a bit like a bell being struck, with the obvious result that seamen got somewhat irritated, and similar salty words were again repeated as part of their encouragement to move us on.

We then came to the part of the quay where there was a slipway. This was an inlet to allow quite large boats to be dragged out of the water and onto the quayside so that they could be cleaned or repaired.

It comprised of a long concrete slope leading from the quayside down to well below the water level and was probably something like fifteen metres wide.

The far side by the river was edged with steps in line with the slope. The top of the ramp was dry but further down it was covered in seaweed, and for the final five metres of the incline toward the water level it was covered in river silt, mainly sand but not now your normal golden colour but more a grey-green shade of mud.

We were just walking past this when Chris noticed that there was something floating in the river about fifteen or so metres out from the quay. Chris then uttered a *"Stay right there and don't move"* order and him and Jacques ran round the outside edge of the slipway, gathering stones on their way and then went down the steps on the far side until they were level with the flotsam and started to aim stones at it.

David, totally ignoring my protests decided to run around collecting stones and putting them in his pockets. I tried to catch Chris or Jacques attention, but either they chose not to hear, or the wind and the river traffic drowned out my calls. David then does no more than jump down onto the *"sandy"* part of the slipway and started to walk across towards them.

When he was almost halfway across he dropped one of the large stones he had in his arms and bend down to pick it up, but that caused him to drop more.

There he was trying to gather his stones back up, but he was sinking into the sand. When he went to move he found his feet stuck and in trying to lift them dropped the stones again. It was not long before he was up to his knees in the mud and despite my continuous yelling I still could not attract the others attention.

I watched as he sunk deeper into the mud, and I

started to get worried. I then thought I had better give him a hand and rushed over to where he was, to give assistance. By which time he was in well past his knees and despite my protestations was determined to keep the stones he had gathered as missiles.

I was petrified this putrid smelling squelchy mud was about to completely swallow him up and I would be left watching as his head disappeared below the surface of the mud. Whereas at that moment he was far more concerned about holding on to the missiles he had previously gathered than his own wellbeing.

As we sank deeper he began to grasp the extent of his plight and then, but only then, did he agree to jettison this extra weight.

However, this had little effect and as we both struggled to free ourselves from this putrid mud we just sunk deeper together, with him in up to his thighs, and me entrapped up to my knees. I was now absolutely distressed we would soon be completely enveloped and even David had started to show concern for us both.

Meanwhile, Chris and Jacques were still happily bombarding the flotsam as the flow of the current took it even further upriver, such that they were now totally out of earshot, almost out of sight, completely unconcerned and oblivious to our pending demise.

Luckily, for us the ferryman, (remember him?) came running to our aid, simply bent down, grabbed David round the waist, told him to hold on to the saviour's neck and such was his size and strength, with one big heave he yanked him out, he then did likewise for me.

As he placed us safely back on the quay he pointed to a very prominent sign that said, *"Danger Quick Sands."*

He then lectured us on the dangers of rivers and recognising us, asked where our mother was and what we were doing there on our own.

We explained and pointed out Chris and Jacques who by then were just distant figures lobbing stones and still totally oblivious to our previous plight. The ferryman then chased up to them, and although I could not hear what he was saying, his distant booming voice and animated arm waving seemed to show he was giving them a thorough piece of his mind.

I am not sure how long after this it was before we crossed the river by ferry again, but mum got a full rundown of the event when we did. He told her we were so lucky that he was returning from lunch and on his way back to his boat, which was moored at the ferry landing and that was a considerable distance away.

Had he not, it is unlikely he would have seen our dilemma and I dread to think what might have happened without his timely intervention.

When Chris and Jacques arrived back with us, Chris was livid that he had to endure the ferryman's wrath and angrily gave us both a like measure of what he had just suffered from the ferryman.

I was dumbfounded, but this was typical of Chris. To his mind the fault lay not with him but with us.

In some respects, maybe he was right, because his point being, had we stayed where instructed it would not have happened. Whereas mine was he had fervently pleaded that he was now mature enough to supervise and protect us, but clearly he was not.

Bearing in mind our ages and probably more importantly our known history he had still willingly

244

taken charge of controlling and safeguarding us. He should have realised that we were far too young and immature to be left without close supervision. Sorry Chris I rest my case.

Anyway, in our futile attempts to disgorge ourselves from a liquid death sentence, we had managed to fully encase ourselves in this foul-smelling mud. There we were, two mud caked, pitiful little individuals trapsing home with passers-by giving us long curious looks and an extremely wide berth, as did Chris and Jacques

As soon as we arrived home, Jacques suddenly and conveniently remembered a prior engagement and set up a world sprint record in his attempt to get to it. Chris knocked on the front door and without hesitation disappeared, breaking Jacque's sprint record by a substantial margin. When Mum opened the door she just stood aghast and motionless in shock before uttering *"Oh my god, what the hell have you done this time"* then with concern added *"Where's Chris."* We just pointed toward the rapidly disappearing distant figure. Obviously, he had decided that cowardice dictated that an explanation was far better left until later when the heat had cooled. Covering her face to shield her from the stench Mum added *"Go round the back through the coal shed."* Once we were out the back of the house she just stood there for a while wondering how to deal with this unbelievable rancid mess. Thinking that there was only one way to effectively deal with this, she told us to strip naked and stand there side by side until we had been hosed off completely using the garden hose.

I am just so glad they didn't have a power washer otherwise I'm sure, with the mood she was in, she would willingly have stripped our skin off too. As if that wasn't enough, we were then taken inside to be given a thorough bath with a great deal of disinfectant added.

Had it not been mid-afternoon I'm sure we would have been packed off to bed there and then. Once we were clean and dry, instead of gently placing clean clothes on our beds for us to put on they were roughly tossed at us, showing that it was likely to be a while before the incident would be forgiven. Thank you Dave! or should I blame Chris!

She then went back out into the rose garden, stayed downwind of the stench, and holding the clothes at arm's length with her washing tongs, hosed them off, immediately put them all in the dustbin and put the lid on tightly. Obviously, Dad had a lot to say about it when he got home and although he really laid it on the line as usual he never singled out anyone, it was again a collective dressing down.

Despite this Chris was indignant at being included because to his mind it was mine and David's fault for not staying where instructed that was the root cause of this calamitous event. Dad then dismissed David and me while he tried to get Chris to understand that because he accepted the overseer duties he was equally to blame for not supervising us while he was away playing with his friend, totally oblivious to our plight. Chris as usual would not listen and stormed off, adamant that he was totally blameless. That was Chris, never ever wrong!

Although I have many more recollections of our early life I have exhausted those that relate to our time in Great Yarmouth, so it is time to end this edition of the tales related to our lives there.

Before concluding I do have to say that the amazing thing is that I cannot remember very much about us packing up our Great Yarmouth home to move to London. However, David recalls it vividly. Given that between us we can recall a great deal of our daily activities related to that period in our early lives, how this event does not rank somewhere higher in my own mind is a complete mystery to me. I cannot understand how such a momentous event as moving our lives, not just to another house, but also a new town many miles from our previous home, completely faded from my own memory. That said, David reminded me that us boys tucked in to help dad build wooden crates for his tools and assist with packing other items into tea chests that dad had obtained. David then mentioned that the removers were Freeborn's of North London and a penny dropped because suddenly I had this vision of this cream coloured removal lorry with its ramp down sitting in the kerb outside our Beccles Road house.

David's recollection is of Dad and Chris riding in the driver's cab while Mum, Anne, David, and I were in the area above the cab of Freeborn's removal lorry, a bit like sitting up front on the top deck of a double decker bus. What is really strange is that sadly the one and only thing I can remember about this whole journey was when we were close to the end of it, and that was seeing that the streetlamps gave off yellow light. I had never seen this before and I did not understand why they were that colour. Of course, I now know they were sodium vapour lamps. These were far more energy efficient than any other at the time. The downside being the light appeared to alter the colour of the surroundings.

This may have reduced the energy bills for many councils, but it certainly made everything *look drab and lacking in dimension*. I sincerely hope this will not be your assessment too, should you choose to review this book.

Anyway, back to the move, what I do know, was that Mum, Anne, David and I were to be temporarily housed in Nanny Gast's top floor flat in Highgate, whereas Dad and Chris went to Auntie Julies house in Wood Green and this is where we have to leave it.

Nevertheless, at some time during 6th December 1952 a removal van stopped outside our new home in Enfield, and there we were entering into a new phase in our lives.

This episode of our lives started and finished in Great Yarmouth. As you have just discovered it began well and then went progressively downhill. From the good times with the garage and financial security, through to fighting daily for every penny, all made just a little more difficult due to the carelessly discarded matches, uncontrollable urban menagerie, and even more so by the unmanageable children. Nevertheless, we managed to survive until finally 'run out of town' by the shear enormity of it all.

Before I finish I have to say, like most families every member has their own unique character and diverse chinks in their makeup and ours is no different. It is the variety of their personalities that makes them very often totally annoying, sometimes interesting and continually dissimilar in character as it is possible for people to be, but there again always loveable as individuals and forever a member of a close-knit family.

I hope you will agree I had at least ten reasons to kill either of my brothers or for them to kill me, despite which we have all remained loved by each other in equal measure throughout our entire lives.

That's families for you.

I admit this is a very strange way to finish the book.
I hope you enjoyed.
Look out for episode two

Printed in Great Britain
by Amazon

71589596R00149